Nuclear First Strike

Nuclear First Strike

Consequences of a Broken Taboo

George H. Quester

The Johns Hopkins University Press
Baltimore

The Johns Hopkins University Press
2715 North Charles Street
Baltimore, Maryland 21218-4363
www.press.jhu.edu

Library of Congress Cataloging-in-Publication Data

Quester, George H.
  Nuclear first strike : consequences of a broken taboo / George H.
Quester.
       p.   cm.
  Includes bibliographical references and index.
  ISBN 0-8018-8284-2 (hardcover : alk. paper)—ISBN 0-8018-
8285-0 (pbk. : alk. paper)
  1. Nuclear warfare. 2. First strike (Nuclear strategy). 3. Military
policy—United States. I. Title.
  U263.Q47 2006
  355.02′17—dc22   2005012138

A catalog record for this book is available from the British Library.

For Liliana, Nicolas, and Oscar

Contents

Preface

I owe many thanks for help in the writing of this book to two anonymous reviewers of the manuscript for Johns Hopkins University Press, to all the people who got trapped into substantive discussions when they simply asked the innocent question "What are you working on now?" and especially to a long series of colleagues and other seminar participants at the University of Maryland and at two dozen other universities and research centers. Todd Lowery and Gil Peleg were very helpful as research assistants.

The book is an expansion and major revision of an exploratory study done with support from the Office of Net Assessment in the United States Department of Defense. The completion of the book, entailing a trying-out of the arguments in seminars around the United States and at a series of international security-oriented institutes around the globe, was facilitated by a grant from the Smith Richardson Foundation. Neither of these organizations is, of course, in any way responsible for the views expressed in this book. A version of Chapter 1 was published in the Spring 2005 issue of *Naval War College Review*.

As always, I am also indebted for the patience and support of my spouse, Aline Olson Quester, who has probably sat through presentations of the depressing scenarios in this book more than she really needed to, but who always makes things more fun.

Nuclear First Strike

Considering the Consequences of Nuclear Weapons Use

As we contemplate the multitude of calamities that might happen in our world, very few seem as dreadful as another use of nuclear weapons in an attack on a city, or anywhere else. Because this prospect is indeed so horrible, relatively few people are ready to focus on it, to consider what would happen next.

This book is intended to survey the probable consequences if nuclear weapons were to be used again in anger, for the first time since the bombing of Nagasaki in 1945. It is a speculative analysis of what the world's likely reactions would be and of what the policy responses of the United States (and the other democracies) perhaps *should* be to such an awful event.

The very worst breaking of the "nuclear taboo" would, of course, be a thermonuclear World War III, from which human life might never recover. The end of the Cold War has led most of us to conclude that the risks of such a nuclear holocaust are much reduced. This book assumes that to be true and therefore mostly addresses the many other ways in which nuclear weapons could again come into use (even while a thermonuclear exchange between the United States and Russia cannot be rated as totally impossible).

Chapter 2 attempts to categorize and pull together some of the many ways in which such a use of nuclear weapons could occur. Chapters 3 and 4 sort the likely world reactions, and likely popular American reactions, to such an escalation. Chapter 5 puts forward some ideas on appropriate policy responses, and Chapter 6 adds some final thoughts.

Rather than detailing the *physical* damage that would be inflicted in various kinds of a nuclear attack, which has been done many times since the onset of the Cold War,[1] this book is a speculative exploration of the political, psychological, and social aftermath of the use of such weapons.

First, however, this introduction will outline some general bounds to the probabilities.

Pessimism or Optimism?

To begin, this book is *not* premised on a pessimistic assumption that another use of nuclear weapons is very likely to occur. Instead, the entire study is based on the prudent assumption that it would be useful to have considered the consequences *if* such an event occurred, on the premise that a total surprise and lack of advance speculation would lead to less-than-optimal policy responses.

Anyone embarking on this kind of speculation, however, runs the risk of being accused of pessimism, or indeed of *favoring* an early erasure of the "nuclear taboo," the stigma that has kept such weapons from being used again, even though a great many have been produced during the past sixty years.

At the minimum, someone opening up this question for analysis will be accused of risking the launching of a self-confirming hypothesis, in which the mere idea of such warfare leads someone else to anticipate such use, which in turn makes such an event more likely all around the system.

Yet it has to be noted that the nuclear weapons question has been shaped by *self-denying* as well as by self-confirming hypotheses. The mere thought of a use of nuclear weapons, and of the damage that such weapons would cause, has driven many governments to devote extra effort to preventing their proliferation and use. If the outlines to be presented in this study were to do nothing more than *reinforce* the nuclear taboo, by making states more ready for any violation of it and better prepared to deter such a violation, the entire exercise would be of value.

It will, therefore, be desirable to avoid excessively speculative analysis, while it will at the same time be important to broaden the horizon of the possibilities being considered. It will be important to note the *most likely* scenarios, while not ignoring those that are less likely and that might thus catch the world more by surprise. And it will be necessary to note the background factors that shape the entire array of possibilities being surveyed here.

Important Background Factors

First, the generally reduced incidence of normal inter-state war must be noted; most current uses of military force are within the boundaries of an established country rather than back and forth across the borders of states.[2] The continuing evolution of economic interdependence, necessary for the prosperity of the world, has imposed a greater price on war in general, in some cases erecting disincentives to war that could even be labeled "economic deterrence."[3] Some analysts have carried this so far as to predict that military force will lose its utility as nations around the world become more concerned with becoming wealthy than with exercising power over each other.[4]

As an additional reinforcement for peace, the rebuff of Saddam Hussein's aggression against Kuwait in 1991 might have been seen as the realization of the collective security system Woodrow Wilson envisaged in 1918 in the League of Nations. Skepticism abounds about the ability of such a system to work effectively enough actually to discourage aggressors, but President George H. W. Bush's rallying of the world to the expulsion of the Iraqis from Kuwait seemed to demonstrate a certain world resolve, to the extent that there have been no such blatant aggressions since 1990.[5]

Yet, any such optimism about a "world without war" still has more than a few obstacles to overcome.[6] India's and Pakistan's nuclear detonations of 1998 demonstrate that the processes of nuclear proliferation have not been totally contained. While Indians and Pakistanis are adept at reciting theories of mutual deterrence, arguing that they can maintain this process of a non-use of weapons just as well as Moscow and Washington managed it after 1949, it can hardly be doubted that their decision to acquire nuclear weapons has been accompanied by thoughts in Islamabad and New Delhi about *using* the weapons.[7]

Also grounds for pessimism, of course, are the events of September 11, 2001, events which occurred after this study was initiated. If the attacks on the World Trade Center and the Pentagon imposed no other shock on our normal ways of thinking, they surely bring into question the notion that military force has become so irrelevant. One would have to be extremely optimistic to conclude in the face of these terrorist attacks, on buildings normally housing some 65,000 people, that terrorist use of *nuclear* weapons is not more likely—if such weapons were ever to slip into terrorist hands. The highjacking of four commercial airliners, to be used in effect as guided missiles in the attacks on such buildings, caught the world by surprise, as the willingness of the terrorists to commit suicide in the United States had not been anticipated and as the vulnerability of buildings like the World Trade Center to the explosive power of the jet fuel on such airliners had not been taken enough into account.[8]

One could, of course, argue that these were "conventional" attacks, since no nuclear, chemical, or biological weapons were involved. Yet the number of human beings put at risk in these attacks might easily qualify as using "weapons of mass destruction."

If the September 11 attacks are added to the hypothetical events examined in this study, most of us would have to conclude that the risks of a terrorist use of nuclear weapons has increased. If one wishes to find any reinforcement for the nuclear taboo here, it might come only in the tone of the American public and congressional response to the horrible events of September 11, for one heard little or no reference to American nuclear options as a possible response to the terrorist attack. More Americans were killed in New York and Washington than had been killed at Pearl Harbor, yet the American inclination was still to avoid nuclear escalation.

In the post–September 11 climate, the failure of Saddam Hussein to open Iraq convincingly enough to the inspectors charged with certifying the absence of weapons of mass destruction, nuclear, chemical, or biological, then led the United States to take the military initiative in 2003, launching a preventive war to occupy all of Iraq and impose a regime change on that country. Fears were expressed in advance that Saddam Hussein's regime might use chemical or biological weapons against advancing American forces, and there was speculation on whether the United States response to such an Iraqi action would involve the use of nuclear weapons, but no such introduction of Iraqi weapons of mass destruction (WMD) occurred.[9]

The net impact of 9/11 and the American response was thus not to raise expectations that the nuclear taboo would soon be broken. But at the same time, the sequence highlighted a general risk that nuclear weapons would be spreading, creating a greater ultimate risk that they would be used; Iran and North Korea, the remaining components of what George W. Bush called the "axis of evil," might perhaps now be accelerating their own pursuit of such weapons, if only in the fear that the American invasion of Iraq threatened other states with a "regime change" if they did not have a sure and reliable nuclear deterrent to hold the Americans back.[10]

The Most Likely Scenarios

It may be useful to note what have been perceived as the *most* likely uses of nuclear weapons, even as we survey the many other possibilities that emerge here. The three most likely cases, for the moment, would have to be an escalation of warfare between Pakistan and India, a capricious action by North Korea, and a terrorist attack on the United States.

If a war breaks out between two opposing nuclear powers, such as today's India and Pakistan, or between some other nuclear dyad of the future, this might be the result of a brinksmanship in which neither side backed down, bluffs got called, and the worst that was threatened became an awful reality. In the aftermath of such a failure in crisis diplomacy, there are at least two broad streams of follow-on.

The worst, of course, would be a process of all-out escalation, a war of rounds fired by both sides until one arsenal or another was exhausted and/or until all the cities of one or both adversaries had been destroyed. In this occasion, the need for intervention by the United States or another outside power might come to seem urgent, lest millions of people be killed day after day.

At the other, more hopeful, extreme, the opposing sides might themselves be so shocked by the magnitude of just one nuclear detonation that they would immediately devote a major effort to achieving a truce and cease-fire, with the role of the outside world being more simply that of a truce facilitator.

The history of past wars does not settle us definitely into either of these flows of events, however. World War I did not involve weapons of mass destruction, but it did impose mass destruction by ordinary weapons, once the unthinkable had happened and the line had been crossed into actual warfare; and it then proved impossible for the warring parties, or outside powers, to achieve a cease-fire. The American decision to enter that war in 1917 could well be seen as an intervention driven by the felt need to end the war more than by a definite identification with one side over the other.

Yet, on a more positive note, the history of successful nuclear deterrence suggests that nations have indeed been in awe of nuclear weapons, have been deterred by the prospect of their use, even while they were intent on deterring their adversaries as well. Would the nations that have been so successfully deterred (since Nagasaki) from using nuclear weapons not then be stopped in their tracks once deterrence had failed, once the anticipated horror of the nuclear destruction of even a single city had come to be realized?[11]

Another of the more probable scenarios is a use of such weapons by North Korea (DPRK), perhaps not quite as "undeterrable" an actor as the suicidal pilots of September 11, but with calculations whose rationales are often very difficult to sort out. This could come in the form of a North Korean nuclear attack against Japan or South Korea or even the United States.[12]

The nearest targets for a North Korean nuclear weapon would be South Korea and Japan, but there are many complications to Pyongyang's using such weapons against either target. If the complications were so severe as to block out the idea of a DPRK nuclear escalation entirely, the world might heave a sigh of relief that Pyongyang might not be so "undeterrable." But the style of the North Korean leadership has unfortunately been such that almost nothing can be excluded.

For Pyongyang to use nuclear weapons to destroy Seoul or another South Korean city would be to kill a great number of Korean "countrymen," the people that the Communist regime has always claimed to identify with and want to liberate. It would also be to destroy a very valuable economic asset which the DPRK has always wanted to capture and the source of economic relief to end the North's material misery.

But, while the Communist leadership of the North has always claimed to love the Korean cousins in the South, Koreans in general have often voiced a hatred for the Japanese, based on the historical memories and experience of Tokyo's forty-year occupation of Korea and on the failure of the current Japanese government to accept the guilt or blame for this very fully, in new editions of schoolbooks, in speeches by public officials, and the like.

For the DPRK to destroy a Japanese city would also be to kill some number of overseas Koreans (a fraction of whom have been identifying with the North Korean regime and remitting substantial amounts of hard currency and material aid to the North), even as it killed a much greater number of Japanese, for whom no affection is evident. Yet the world's outrage at a DPRK nuclear attack would surely be increased if the target were *Japan,* the only victim in history of such an attack, a victim for which there would thus inevitably be a reinforced wave of sympathy.

Unless the circumstances are extraordinarily peculiar, the world is thus very likely to denounce, and to be ready to back strong actions against, *any* use of nuclear weapons by Pyongyang. But this reaction could be counted upon to be all the more vehement if Japan were the target, if Japan had to suffer again.

Based on the seeming irrationality of Pyongyang's past behavior, the Japanese public has been quite sensitive to the possibility of North Korea's acquiring nuclear warheads or developing the missiles to deliver them to a Japanese target. Yet it has had to live for a longer time with the fact that Communist China acquired nuclear weapons and had the delivery systems needed to reach Japan during a period when Beijing at times seemed almost as irrationally disposed toward the outside world as Pyongyang seems today. (It must be noted that Beijing once fit all the dimensions of a "rogue state.") There is also still a strong anti-Japanese feeling among the Chinese people, comparable to what one sees among the Koreans.

The trend in Japanese politics and in Japanese military procurement decisions, in face of such nuclear threats, is thus not so easy to predict. In one version, as long as no nuclear weapons were *used* anywhere, even if Pyongyang kept on testing missiles and openly acquired nuclear warheads, Japan would simply continue relying on the American connection, or world opinion, or something else to deter any North Korean attack. A very different version of the future would see Japan moving to acquire nuclear weapons of its own.[13]

Many other scenarios remain. Perhaps as part of an escalation between India and Pakistan, or even without it, there remains an inherent risk of a nuclear exchange between India and *China*.

Moving westward, in a certain broad sense the existence of Israel is continually in danger, because of the hostility of its Arab neighbors and because of the narrowness of its boundaries, which always pose some doubt about the reliability of a conventional defense. While the rumors of Israel's possessing nuclear weapons have served as insurance for Israeli security over the past four decades, one can never rule out the possibility of their coming into *use*.[14]

One must also take into account the bombastic statements that sometimes emerge from Iranian and other pulpits, whereby an Islamic nuclear weapon would be the means for destroying Israel in a single strike by destroying its cities and killing its people.[15] Such a horrendous scenario might be muted by concern for the safety of Jerusalem, one of the three holiest sites for any Muslim, and by concern for the safety of Arabs who live in Israel or the West Bank, but the rationality of decision processes in the Middle East has not been reassuring to the outside world.

The likely new uses of nuclear weapons must also include an array of insubordinate or outrightly "crazy" nuclear attacks and ones by terrorist groups unaffiliated with any existing government. And the risks even include the possibility that the United States would be the power using such weapons again; for decades the United States kept open the "flexible response" option of introducing nuclear weapons for the defense of NATO or South Korea if a conventional aggression by Communists could not otherwise be repulsed.[16]

Whenever nuclear forces are present in the arsenals of states involved in an international crisis, there is the risk that such weapons will be used if a conventional battle were to erupt, because of the sheer confusion and chaos that emerges in the progress of fighting and because of the natural reactions of any military unit that faces being overrun but has nuclear weapons close at hand.

This inherent risk of escalation played a role in making American nuclear responses credible on behalf of NATO in the decades when the Soviet Union was seen as having the conventional advantage in an invasion of Western Europe. Even if an American president might have found it preferable to avoid introducing nuclear weapons when Warsaw Pact tanks were advancing, American units possessing "tactical" nuclear weapons were deployed in the path of such a Soviet armored advance. There is an old tradition in the artillery units of this world by which one does not allow one's ammunition to be captured, but rather goes down firing it at the enemy; the leadership in Moscow could thus never rule out the possibility that a successful armored advance into Western Europe would have triggered a nuclear response, regardless of an American president's concern to protect American cities.

Some of the same inherent motivations and concerns would be at play in future scenarios of a conventional military conflict between Communist China and the United States about Taiwan. Both Beijing and Washington might therefore find it in their national interests to keep such a conventional war quite limited and to keep nuclear weapons from being introduced. But nuclear warheads might be present on board the warships of either power, and, if such a ship were sunk or just attacked, there is always some risk that the nuclear weapons would be fired before the ship went down.[17]

The mere prospect of such a nuclear escalation might lead either side to tighten up its command-and-control arrangements so substantially that this could not happen, and perhaps to pull the nuclear weapons far back from the locus of any likely confrontation, so that they would be out of harm's way.

The Chinese Communist regime proclaimed a "no-first-use" policy from the moment it had tested its first nuclear weapons, suggesting that it did not want to threaten nuclear escalation but rather to deter any adversary from such escalation.[18]

But the same inherent risks can be exploited to make the other side very cautious about even getting into a conventional war, because of the deterring fear that this might lead to a nuclear holocaust. Thus, in recent years we have seen Chinese defense scholars publishing articles suggesting that the Chinese military might find *some* battlefield uses for nuclear weapons, or might want to brandish the possibility that China would indeed be the first, rather than the second, to employ nuclear weapons once a war had begun.[19] As each side in effect plays "chicken" with such risks, a nuclear escalation could occur, by accident, in the heat of battle.

At the beginning of the twenty-first century, one could envisage only a few such scenarios of warfare in which *both* sides possessed nuclear weapons—the confrontation between Pakistan and India, between India and China, between the United States and China—but there will be more such risks in the future if nuclear weapons continue to spread. For almost all such cases, if a nuclear weapon is actually brought into use, *both* sides are likely to regret the event; deterrence will have failed when one side in the confrontation took enough of a risk to trigger nuclear weapons use by the other.

In the cases mentioned, preexisting crises and conventional confrontations would have prepared the outside world for the possibility of an introduction of nuclear weapons, so that it would come as a little less of a shock than in many of our other scenarios. The immediate target, an American aircraft carrier or Pakistani troop concentration, would be a military target, perhaps thus affronting the world's moral sentiments a little less than if a city had been hit. But the sheer number of sailors or soldiers killed in such an escalation would nonetheless still be a major shock to the world.

For a variety of reasons, the natural response of the victim of such an attack would be to hit back with a nuclear retaliation, amid the risk that such a nuclear exchange would quickly get out of hand and target major cities.

The net impact of the mere presence of nuclear weapons has been similar to that achieved in the Cold War, when conventional warfare was thus discouraged, or at least more carefully managed. Their mere presence nevertheless risks the first use of them since Nagasaki.

The Less Likely Scenarios

We must also be on guard against a nuclear attack that comes in a much less anticipated *form*. What we expect the least may cause us the greatest damage and shock, if and when it occurs. The many different ways that nuclear weapons could again come into use range from the very major to the more minor. The cases we have to be prepared for include multiple nuclear strikes or a single detonation. The latter could be accompanied by clear signals that more such attacks were coming, but if a single detonation were followed by signals that *nothing* else was threatened for the moment, the world's reactions would be considerably different from those following more sizable nuclear attacks. As to the physical impact of such an event, one can envisage nuclear escalations in which *no one* gets killed and escalations in which *millions* perish.

In predicting the likely reactions of the world and for sorting out the presumably best policy responses for the United States, much will thus depend on whether the damage inflicted in the initial nuclear weapons use seems to be containable (and perhaps even preventible in the future, if proper new defensive steps are taken), or whether it instead seems to be open-ended. If the use looks like a one-time aberration from the post-1945 normal pattern, outside reactions may be calmer, with the situation seeming to be manageable along the same broad lines followed since World War II. But if it looks like the door on nuclear destructiveness cannot be locked again after this first round, much larger and urgent responsive steps may seem in order.

Weapons systems of various sorts are proliferating worldwide, and much may depend on what kinds of systems, offensive ones or defensive, have already been deployed by the time a nuclear weapon is used. A great number of relevant possibilities have to be introduced here. By the time of such a nuclear escalation, the United States may already have effective missile defenses and resuscitated air defenses, or it may not, despite vast expenditures on such systems; and there may or may not have been a widespread proliferation of chemical and biological weapons in the world.[20]

As in all the wars and war plans of the past, much will depend on what kinds of targets are hit. Nuclear weapons are most often thought of as a "countervalue" weapon, capable of destroying entire cities, as at Hiroshima and Nagasaki; but contingencies have existed, ever since the onset of the Cold War, for much more strictly countermilitary or counterforce uses of nuclear weapons.[21] Again, there may be a great variation in the results achieved in such a more specific attack. If important military goals were achieved in the escalation, very different responses might emerge than if the nuclear escalation proved relatively fruitless.

Who the actor is would play a critical role in the perception of the event. The next power to use a nuclear weapon in combat could be a state hostile to the United States; to the extent that Americans have been thinking about this problem at all, this is the scenario that naturally captures the most attention. But the user could instead be a power which is neither hostile nor friendly to the United States, the use being part of a conflict in which it would be difficult for Americans to identify with either side. The nuclear escalator might even be an ally of the United States. Finally, as noted, the scenarios for the next use of nuclear weapons must also include those involving such action by United States armed forces.

The *victim* of a next nuclear attack might be the United States itself, an American territory, an American military base abroad, or ships of the United States Navy. Or the victim might be a state closely allied with the United States, a military ally, or a state which for historical and cultural reasons is regarded with particular friendship by Americans. Alternatively, the nuclear escalation could come where the United States does not feel particular pain at the victimization of either side or the victim might be a state seen as an enemy by the United States, a foreign country (to cite an example, Iran) whose government, and perhaps even most of whose people, had been viewed as hostile to Americans in the months and years before this escalation. (If the destruction in the nuclear attack brought extensive and vivid coverage by CNN or its equivalent, this might add some sympathetic identification, of course, even if there would otherwise have been a more indifferent American attitude.)[22]

The country using the nuclear weapon, and/or the victim, might have an extensive following around the world, a linkage of ethnicity or ideology that would produce a widespread sympathy. Two obvious examples would be an Islamic regime, and a radical, perhaps Marxist, regime, which might be viewed elsewhere as representing the economically downtrodden of the world. By comparison, the perpetrator, or the victim, of a nuclear attack might be a state that is relatively off-by-itself in terms of any identification with many other states (Israel or India being plausible examples).

Yet another category of difference in the scenarios relates to the motivation for nuclear weapons use. The scenarios here include someone else's use of another kind of weapon of mass destruction, chemical or biological, or someone else's launching of a major conventional military attack.[23]

Or the nuclear escalation might not have been a response to any external event at all and might not have reflected any conscious decision by the government whose weapons were detonated; it might instead have been an act of insubordination or insanity or an act by a terrorist movement with no following and no territory to control, an escalation perhaps intended to damage the very government whose nuclear weapons were put into use.

Differences in the style of planning of the act could range from carefully calculated and centrally managed to possibilities of systems going berserk. Especially in a counterforce action, the decision might be driven by anticipation of a comparable attack from the other side, basically thus becoming a preemptive attack, with all the tension and mutual reinforcement of tension that such preemptive scenarios have always included.

Some victims of nuclear attack might be seen by most of the world as very innocent of any wrongdoing, of anything that might justify such an attack, while others might seem much more "guilty" by one standard or another, that is, more understandably the target of someone's desire for retribution. If the nuclear attack came after a prolonged and very destructive conventional war in which hundreds of thousands of people had already become casualties (as in August 1945), the outside-world shock at a nuclear escalation would be much less. Shock and indignation are very much a matter of previous expectations and context.

The Nature of a Taboo

One often hears references to the "taboo" on the use of nuclear weapons, but people usually have some difficulty in putting their finger on exactly what they mean by this term.[24] A taboo surely is more than simply something we would want to avoid, something that we disapprove of, for we do not hear of a taboo on bank robberies or a taboo on murder. The word is distinctive in that it refers to something that we are not willing even to think about doing. There is no weighing of benefits and costs; we simply reject the idea without further thought.

The best example in ordinary life is the taboo on incest. If our six-year-old daughter asks whether she can marry her brother when they grow up, we as parents typically do not reason with the child by noting, "Your brother and you are always squabbling about your toys; surely you can find someone else more compatible to marry." We instead respond simply, "No one marries their brother or sister!" and the child quickly picks up the signal that this is something that is simply not done.

Another taboo is cannibalism. Air force crews are briefed on hundreds of measures they can take to survive after a crash, but one subject *never* touched is how one would avoid starvation by consuming the body of a dead comrade. The entire question is just not thinkable.

The attitude toward using nuclear weapons that seems to have settled into place over the more than fifty years since Nagasaki may indeed have taken the form of a taboo, as we do not hear many discussions of the costs and benefits of a nuclear escalation but often encounter a somewhat unchallenged conclusion that such escalation is simply out of the question.

Similarly, one hears about the development of a "customary international law" by which the battlefield application of nuclear weapons has become somehow illegal, although without any international treaties having been signed and ratified, simply because we have gone this long without using them.[25]

How such a custom or taboo develops and what happens to it when it is violated will play an important part in our assessment of what the world will be like after a new nuclear attack. If nuclear weapons do not get used again in anger for decade after decade, this in some ways strengthens the taboo, but there are also a few ways in which the disuse may endanger the taboo.

The reinforcement comes simply from the general sense that this must be unthinkable because no one has initiated such an act for so long; a form of "customary international law" settles into place by which the abstinence from an act presses all states to abstain. People did not begin speaking about a "nuclear taboo" for a number of years after Nagasaki. It was only in the later 1950s, after more than a decade had passed without a repetition of the experiences of Hiroshima and Nagasaki that the sense emerged that a barrier now existed to treating nuclear weapons as "just another weapon."[26]

But the counter to this might emerge, once there is hardly anyone alive anymore who was a victim of the 1945 attacks or who remembers seeing the immediate photographs of these victims, or anyone who remembers the nuclear testing programs of the 1950s and 1960s. The bans on nuclear testing have been intended to shield the environment and to discourage horizontal and vertical nuclear proliferation. But an unwelcome result of these test bans is that some of the perceived horror of such weapons may fade, so that ordinary human beings will be a little less primed to react automatically against the idea of their use.

The only circumstance that can fairly test the long-term viability of the nuclear taboo will, of course, be for the world to manage to keep that taboo observed and intact. The net trend, the net result, of a prolongation of the pattern of non-use is *most probably* that such non-use will be strengthened and renewed thereby, just as it seems to have been over the decades of the Cold War and its aftermath.

There are parallel taboos on types of warfare which are still observed by most states, although they have been violated in the last several decades. The world for many years sensed a taboo on chemical warfare, reinforced by the Geneva Protocol but observed even by states which had not yet ratified the protocol (the best example being the United States at its entry into World War II). A similar taboo-like aversion is thought to apply to biological warfare.[27] The long period in which naval forces did not engage each other on the high seas (broken only by the Argentine-British war over the Falklands) may have some similar characteristics. Generally, it seems that the longer we go without engaging in a form of warfare, the stranger and less manageable that kind of conflict will seem and the more the public and others will regard it as simply not to be contemplated.

At times, resistance to the proliferation of nuclear weapons has seemed to be mobilizing a worldwide popular feeling that there was a taboo or customary international law against proliferation as well, that ordinary people and even military professionals in many countries were coming to assume that nuclear weapons were so horrible, and so different, that it simply made no sense to think of even acquiring them.[28]

One more kind of taboo on weapons use, grossly violated in the attacks on the United States beginning on September 11, was a pattern, not easily explained while it persisted, by which terrorists had not engaged in attacks using weapons of mass destruction. Analysts of terrorism used to wrestle with why terrorist attacks had thus far never threatened more than dozens or, rarely, hundreds of innocent people and had not utilized chemical or biological weapons.[29] Some argued that the chemical and biological weapons were too difficult to acquire, while other experts in these areas of science scoffed, suggesting that their first-year graduate students were up to the task of producing such weapons.

The explanations then tended to shift to the motivation of the terrorists, by which they might be seeking to win the sympathies of the populations on which they were inflicting their attacks. With regard to WMD, some analysts suggested that terrorists might have been imitating governments, perhaps because they were seeking to become governments themselves. Since governments were not using chemical and biological weapons, this perhaps explained why terrorists were not using them either, as they were affected by some of the same cultural norms, by the same taboo. And since governments were not killing thousands of people in nuclear exchanges, the terrorists would perhaps similarly be steered away from using such weapons.

All of these assumptions were, of course, very badly shaken after September 11, as the airliners that were seized and flown into huge buildings put more than 65,000 people at risk, and as the use of anthrax in letters mailed to various public figures introduced a biological warfare element into terrorism,[30] just as the 1995 nerve gas attack on the Tokyo subway by the Aum Shinrikyo cult had introduced the chemical weapons element.[31]

When taboos are thus violated, the question immediately arises whether they will remain as taboos, or whether the violation will make the same actions by many other parties much more thinkable. We may be able to learn something from the aftermath of the cases where other taboos were violated. The world has seen several rounds of chemical warfare since the 1950s, even though this was the one kind of warfare the Allies and the Axis basically managed to abstain from during World War II.[32] There have been reports that the Soviet Union and its allies experimented with various forms of biological warfare in Cambodia and in Afghanistan, and the Japanese are known to have engaged in horrible experiments with biological warfare during World War II in China.[33] Yet, most of the world still regards chemical and biological warfare as rather "unthinkable," not something to be weighed in terms of costs and gains.

The Indian and Pakistani detonations of nuclear warheads in 1998 may not have changed very much of the *reality* of whether there was nuclear proliferation under way in South Asia, as India was projected to have enough plutonium for as many as seventy-five nuclear weapons and had already detonated a "peaceful nuclear explosive" in 1974, and as Pakistan was assumed to have enough enriched uranium for as many as ten warheads.[34] But the blatant detonation challenged the idea that a further spread of nuclear weapons was unthinkable, that it was some kind of a taboo.

Pessimists might have expected extensive nuclear weapons proliferation around the world after India and Pakistan had made such an open display of their acquisition of such weapons, and such pessimists might similarly have expected numerous incidents of high-seas warfare after the Falklands War. Fortunately for the world, neither has happened. When we speculate here about the aftermath of a violation of the *nuclear* taboo, some lessons may thus be extractable from these parallels, where a single violation has not totally shattered the pattern of restraint or eliminated the world public opinion behind that restraint.

Pessimists might expect that the use of chemical and biological warfare is now generally more likely, as more and more states and even non-state actors are able to lay their hands on such weapons, as the instances of state and non-state exploitation of such weapons erode the taboo. One has to be very careful not to ignore the pessimistic forecasts—just as one has to expect that the attacks on the World Trade Center will not be one-of-a-kind operations just because the immediate perpetrators killed themselves in the process of executing the attacks. Other attacks are likely to be launched against tall buildings, by agents of the same organization that launched the September 11 attacks or by "copy-cat" imitators.

Yet, while taking the pessimistic possibilities into account, one should also not simply conclude that nothing good is possible thereafter, that the world's feelings about what is thinkable or unthinkable would make no difference. If nuclear weapons are used, whatever taboo is at work will indeed have been violated, with the probability that other uses of such weapons will then seem more thinkable. Yet the very possibility that a taboo had been in place might suggest that it can be renewed and retained. If most of the world has regarded some kind of military action as unthinkable, the actual occurrence of such an action challenges such an attitude but does not necessarily demolish it.

Near-Misses of the Past

It is sometimes thought that useful perspectives on the world after a nuclear weapons use might be gained from studying the "near-misses" of the past. Many regard the Cuban missile crisis as the point in the Cold War when we came closest to nuclear war.[35] Others point to Israeli decision making after the 1973 Egyptian Yom Kippur attack.[36] More recently, we have seen rumors that the British Navy may have had nuclear weapons on board some of the ships engaged in the recovery of the Falklands in the South Atlantic war of 1982;[37] and there has been speculation about whether Iraq might have possessed enough fissionable material to put together one nuclear warhead at the time of its invasion of Kuwait in 1991 and on whether a use of Iraqi chemical or biological weapons against the forces liberating Kuwait might have drawn a nuclear response from the United States, Britain, or France.[38]

Since these were indeed near-misses rather than actual nuclear escalation, we thus have no direct lessons to extract from these cases on what the *aftermath* of a nuclear weapons use would have been. Such cases are nonetheless suggestive, and potentially useful as we compile our initial array of the ways in which a nuclear weapon might be used. If the use of Iraqi chemical or biological WMD had produced retaliation—using the only WMD the United States possesses, nuclear weapons—this would supply one model. If British nuclear depth charges had been used in the Falklands War, because there was no other way to get rid of an Argentine submarine that was threatening the major aircraft carriers or troop ships of the British force, this would have been a quite different model. And, if Israel were to use the nuclear weapons it has long been assumed to have, as a last-gasp retaliation for any prospective Arab victory in conventional tank battles, as its population faced being pushed into the sea, this would of course be yet another model.

Lessons from Simulations

One can learn from simulations of possible scenarios, and one can indeed teach the participants in such simulations a great deal about the choices and options that a national decision maker would face in some future crisis.[39] Yet one can also exaggerate the reliability of such simulations as a research tool and as a predictor of future behavior, because the individuals taking part may be excessively self-conscious about role-playing.

It is a common observation about the many such simulations conducted during the Cold War that the players turned out to be surprisingly reluctant to employ nuclear weapons, that is, reluctant to escalate, even when the scenario was designed to explore what the *nuclear* phase of a war would be like. Such simulations might thus be good news, suggesting that the entire premise of this study is too pessimistic, that nuclear weapons are *not* so likely to come into use. But, alternatively, these simulations might support a more worrisome assumption: that the players in such exercises are themselves simply under the influence of the nuclear taboo, inclined to see a use of such weapons as unthinkable, and hence reinforcing our disinclination to even think about nuclear escalation and its consequences.

If the players in simulations are not ready for nuclear weapons use, it is probable that we are *all* not ready enough for this possibility—all, that is, except for the solitary rogue-state decision maker who one day launches such weapons.

Countervalue or Counterforce Targeting

Since 1945, nuclear weapons have been seen primarily as a "countervalue" instrument, significant for how it affects the motivations of the opposing side rather than for what it can do to its capabilities. It was nuclear weapons that *persuaded* the Japanese to surrender and *persuaded* the Soviets not to exploit their advantage in conventional forces in Europe, rather than crippling the Japanese forces to pave the way for an amphibious invasion of Japan or repelling the Warsaw Pact's arrays of tanks.

All through the Cold War, there were advocates of "tactical," battlefield, applications of nuclear weapons, which would typically require development of more advanced nuclear weapons designs, lower in yield and lighter in weight. Skeptics about the effectiveness of such weapons saw them mainly as "trip wires" designed to do little more than push a conflict over the conventional/nuclear line, leading then to all-out escalation and a World War III, the mere prospect of which would deter the launching of a war in the first place, in Europe or in the Korean Peninsula.

The exploitation of the deterring and compelling power of nuclear weapons was thus *mainly* a story of their being brandished but not used, being held in reserve. Hiroshima and Nagasaki had to suffer actual destruction because we did not yet know what such weapons could do. Some of the nuclear scientists who created them had urged that the first atomic bombs be demonstrated first on some uninhabited island, so that Japan could see what fate was threatened for its cities, without a city actually having to be destroyed. The action would have been a "countervalue" threat against cities, just as with the later thermonuclear weapons demonstrated at Eniwetok, but would have been potential and held in reserve. No Americans really wanted to have Hiroshima or Nagasaki destroyed; they wanted Japan to surrender so

·that such cities could be occupied by American military forces and then democratized.

As we contemplate the prospects of further nuclear weapons use, however, we must consider *real* uses of such weapons, used with the intention to cripple or destroy real targets rather than merely to deter or compel opposing-party behavior. Some of such scenarios will become possible because nuclear warheads will be improved to have lower yields of radioactivity and blast and heat, so that they could serve as effective antitank weapons,[40] destroying less of the surrounding countryside in the process of repulsing an armored attack. Other strands of scenarios will develop because of new motivations for conflict that affect the confrontations between states.

Two current speculations could be cited about nuclear weapons being used actually to *kill* an opponent rather than to intimidate. The case is sometimes made that if the leadership of some terrorist group such as Al Qaeda had buried itself in some deep underground bunker, perhaps a shelter which contained also its rudimentary stockpile of biological weapons, or its first atomic bombs, the advanced deep-penetration nuclear warheads of the United States or some other major power could be legitimately used to dig out and destroy such a bunker.[41] The world would be less likely to condemn, and more likely to applaud, if the next use of nuclear weapons had the effect of preempting a WMD attack against a major population center, heading off a biological attack or a nuclear attack by destroying the implicated weapon of mass destruction before it could be used.

A very different example of this emerging strand of motivation is illustrated in the statements noted earlier of some Iranian strategic commentators, by which an Islamic nuclear weapon would be used to "kill" Israel, not to deter the Israelis or to defeat their military forces, but to solve the Arab problem with Israel once and for all by destroying Tel Aviv, Haifa, and the other Israeli population centers so that the Palestinian Arabs could live the way that they have all along wanted to live, all by themselves in Palestine.[42]

What would have made such a scenario much less thinkable in the past, even from the most hostile Arab or Iranian view, was the fact that a great number of Islamic Arabs would be killed as well in the nuclear attack. The mutual-deterrence relationship between Israel and its Arab enemies has all along been very asymmetrical: Israel could meaningfully threaten to destroy Damascus or Cairo as its retaliation for an Arab conventional military attack, but the Arab states could not pose a parallel threat to Haifa, with its sizable Arab population, or to very much of the rest of Israel, or to Jerusalem, the third holiest site for Islam, also housing a substantial Arab population. The Arabs living close by may have been seen as generally unwelcome by the Israelis, but they served at the same time as hostages limiting the Arab ability to brandish nuclear weapons.

But the Israeli response to Arab conventional suicide bombers and ordinary terrorism may over time be driven to seeking a greater and greater separation of the two populations; some Israeli hard-liners are already suggesting that they would be happiest if most of the Arabs were to move across the Jordan River. If Israelis are persuaded that they would be better off living by themselves, their enemies may feel much more free to think of a nuclear attack as a viable approach.

For a malevolent Iranian or other Islamic nuclear strategist, a problem still to be solved would be the preservation of Jerusalem and the lingering radioactivity on the Palestinian land, once Arabs were finally free to reclaim Jaffa and all the rest of Palestine.

Optimism or Pessimism?

At first this study might seem more interesting to those who are pessimistic about future risks and who might thus regard speculation about an end to the nuclear taboo as very much overdue. Yet the author must repeat that pessimism may not be so necessary here, since an analysis of the likely consequences of nuclear escalation may indeed persuade the relevant governments and publics to head off such escalation.

If asked, prior to this study, to estimate the likelihood of our avoiding further use of nuclear weapons, this author would have guessed that the chances were as good as three out of five that no such event would occur in the period up to 2045, that is, that there was a better-than-even chance that the world would be commemorating a full century of non-use of such weapons since Nagasaki. But, when such a prediction has been put to analysts and ordinary citizens around the world, it has typically been dismissed as "too optimistic." Indeed, the response of such audiences has often been a bit bizarre: replies like "We have not been thinking at all about this topic, about the next use of nuclear weapons, but we think that you are too optimistic about such use being avoided." Responses like this from an audience in Israel or Sweden or Japan, or in the United States, might thus easily enough support the worry that people around the world have simply been repressing an unpleasant reality, have been avoiding thinking about a very real danger. But the possibility also remains that the relative absence of attention to this topic is not simply a repression of reality but rather a reinforcement for the unthinkability of nuclear weapons use.

One could introduce another wedge of hope: that any use of nuclear weapons between now and our suggested commemorative date of 2045 would be followed by reactions and consequences that reinforced rather than eroded the pattern of a taboo, as the perpetrator of the attack would not have advanced its interests by such an escalation but actually lost the battles and territories that were at issue because the world did not retreat in face of such use but rallied to punish it. If a solitary use of nuclear weapons were to be followed by such effective punitive responses, so that *no other* use of such weapons occurred by 2045, the "centenary celebration" might be less grand but still justified, and a basic pattern of optimism rather than pessimism would still be in place.

A very much more pessimistic strand of overall analysis would intrude here to draw attention to other weapons of mass destruction, chemical and biological. By our proposed benchmark year of 2045, the spread of capabilities for such weapons may be so enormous, because of the inherent dual-use nature of the science and technology in these fields, that a great number of nations, and of subnational terrorist groups, may be able to lay their hands on such weapons. If a biological warfare attack can kill more people than were killed at Hiroshima or Nagasaki, might there be little or no accomplishment in a continued pattern of the non-use of *nuclear* weapons?[43]

The speed in the advances of technology also suggests that some entirely new approaches to mass destruction will emerge within the next forty years, involving approaches just as unimaginable now as nuclear physics might have been for almost everyone in the year 1905. The speculation about cyber terrorism at the beginning of this millennium made the Y2K adjustment a useful rehearsal, with the happy result on January 1, 2000, that banking and other important systems did not break down, that the storage of drinking water and other necessities around the globe turned out to have been unnecessary. But specialists on information technology can see ways in which someone intent on disrupting computer networks could do much more damage than merely delaying e-mail transmissions or ATM operations, indeed causing major explosions and killing large numbers of people.

Yet none of the speculation about the unfolding array of approaches to mass destruction—chemical, biological, computer hacking, or exploiting entirely new realms of science—negates the existing destructive potential of nuclear and thermonuclear weapons. None of such possibilities as yet negates the premise that we would all be profoundly shocked, well beyond our ability to forecast such shock, by most of the imaginable uses of nuclear weapons. So, avoiding the use of such weapons would indeed still be a major and self-renewing accomplishment.

For the foreseeable future, nuclear weapons thus continue to be uniquely and distinctly threatening as weapons of mass destruction, in the amount of damage they can do and in the rapidity with which they can do it. The threat of *other* WMD does not yet suggest that the nuclear element has lost its relevance or that there is no point in focusing in particular on *nuclear* weapons and whether they will be held back out of use.

We indeed have reason to be horrified by what a smallpox or anthrax attack could inflict on an unprotected population; there are ways in which a biological or chemical attack inspires fears a nuclear attack does not. It might be ambiguous in its earliest symptoms, leaving governments and private citizens quite unsure from day to day whether an attack was even under way, thus generating waves of false alarms, for instance.

Yet, the absence of any nuclear attacks since Nagasaki and the numbing of our feelings through all the Cold War years of preparation for a thermonuclear holocaust may also have caused us to collectively underrate the horror of a nuclear attack on a city. In actual fact, the horror after a nuclear attack will almost certainly be significantly greater than the horror inflicted by any other kind of weapons.

In this context of multiple mass destruction weapons, there are important policy choices to be made. Should nuclear, chemical, and biological weapons be lumped together as "WMD" or should they be handled separately in the nonproliferation efforts aimed at the *acquisition* of such weapons and the deterrence efforts focused on their *use*?[44] The world since 1945 has been relatively successful at handling the dual-use aspect of nuclear technology, by getting under way the safeguards, precedents, and procedures of the International Atomic Energy Agency (IAEA) and by getting most nations to renounce the possession of nuclear weapons for themselves (accepting the principle that they can utilize nuclear technology for peaceful purposes only if they submit such operations to this IAEA international inspection), even while the first five possessors of nuclear weapons continue to possess them.[45] By comparison, the dual-use problems in the chemical and biological fields may be much more difficult to manage.[46] If the accomplishments in *nuclear* nonproliferation were to be diluted, and perhaps squandered, in lumping everything together as a single nonproliferation effort for *all* mass-destruction weapons, this might be a far from optimal choice.

Similarly, a "no-first-use" policy applying specifically to nuclear weapons is something substantially different from a "no-first-use of WMD" policy. The latter may have the benefit of making the introduction of chemical or biological weapons less likely, but it may come at the price of introducing one more scenario in which nuclear weapons could come into use, perhaps even with the United States again being the user.

This study, if for no other good reason than the public imagery involved, takes 2045, the hundredth year after the attack on Nagasaki, as a meaningful landmark. If abstention from nuclear attack can be maintained until then, the "nuclear taboo," the idea that the use of nuclear weapons is unthinkable, will most probably be reinforced. If such an abstention can be maintained, something substantial will indeed have been accomplished.

The Structure of the Argument

Chapter 2 lists some of the vast variety of ways that nuclear weapons could be used again, sorting these into functional categories that might suggest differences in policy response.

Addressing this array of categories, Chapter 3 then speculates about the likely world reactions to such breakings of the nuclear taboo. Chapter 4 speculates similarly about American popular responses. The word *speculate* is used advisedly, since we have *no* experience to go on here; indeed, the easiest prediction to make is that any actual use of nuclear weapons anywhere in the world will shock us all, in a manner that will render us hardly capable of predicting our reactions.

Chapter 5 puts forward this author's suggestions for what would be the better *policy responses* to such events by the American government and by the governments of the other democracies, or any sensible government.

Against the background of so much contingency and uncertainty, the final chapter offers a few conclusions.

CHAPTER TWO

Some Scenarios of Nuclear Escalation

Rather than simply striving to see how many different scenarios one can imagine for a new use of nuclear weapons, this book is intended to find some "differences that make a difference." This chapter will thus begin by grouping the many ways that nuclear weapons could be used into an array of categories that might lead to very different likely reactions by Americans and other people around the world and that might then suggest very different *appropriate* policy responses.

Readers are of course free to sort the many possible forms of nuclear escalation by their own logic, rather than by that represented here. The following are proposed as some discrete and interesting types of scenarios, each of which may suggest policy conclusions that might not have been immediately evident.

A. Cases of ambiguity, because of either uncertainty of definitions or doubts about the facts on whether the nuclear taboo had indeed been violated

B. Cases with minimal or no collateral damage to civilians, in which the weapons were used mostly or entirely against military targets

C. Cases with uncertainty about the responsibility for the decision to strike, ranging from simple accident, to insubordination, to outright madness and nuclear terrorism

D. Clear and highly destructive nuclear escalation, with definite government responsibility, with the world being inclined to retreat thereafter

E. Clear and highly destructive nuclear escalation, with definite government responsibility, launched by a rogue state, but with a braver outside world response

F. Clear and highly destructive nuclear escalation, but in an ongoing contest where two opposing sides are hitting each other with nuclear weapons

G. Clear and highly destructive nuclear escalation, but where the perpetrator retains a major residual nuclear force, with the aftermath perhaps having to take the form of "limited strategic nuclear war"

Ambiguity about Whether the Line Was Crossed (Category A)

A certain number of scenarios of nuclear event will be inherently ambiguous, in the view of the world and the United States government, because of difficulties in establishing the facts or because of important ambiguities of definition, leaving opinion not at all certain whether a nuclear escalation had actually occurred. (An analogy would be our uncertainty about whether it was a nuclear device detonated over the South Atlantic in 1979.)[1] American policy may not be as ready as it should be for such ambiguous cases, and for how to respond to them. One could simply define away the ambiguous cases as nonviolations of the nuclear non-use pattern, thus hoping to avoid the setting of a dangerous precedent; but this may not always be a workable approach, if the ambiguity were bound to clear over time.

There are thus some very marginal forms of "nuclear escalation" which many of us might not even regard as a definitive crossing of the crucial line. The spreading of nuclear "garbage"—radioactive debris—has been speculated about in the past as a tool for terrorists or for countries not yet able to master the actual design of a Hiroshima-type bomb.[2] Making the distinctions similarly more ambiguous would be a conventional attack on a nuclear power plant, with the intent to spread hazardous radioactive materials around the surrounding countryside.[3] Or, as in the Israeli attack on the Iraqi facility at Osirak in 1981, the strike might be straightforwardly intended to preempt someone else's development of nuclear weapons.[4]

The possibility of a conventional attack on one of the nuclear reactors used to produce electrical power has been addressed in the past. India and Pakistan signed a mutual agreement in 1985 promising that neither would attack the reactors of the other, this at a point when India had already test-detonated a "peaceful nuclear explosive" in 1974 and when Pakistan was widely suspected of having acquired enriched uranium to produce atomic bombs of its own, the first test-detonation of which came in 1998.[5] During the Cold War, some West German and other analysts in Western Europe also opened the subject of "nuclear deterrence without nuclear weapons," arguing that the installation of power-producing reactors across West Germany, in the likely path of any advance by the armored forces of the Warsaw Pact, already generated a form of de facto trip wire nuclear deterrence, since the conventional fighting around such reactors would most probably inflict enough damage to release radioactivity eastward, in a pattern dwarfing what occurred at Chernobyl in 1986.

Similarly ambiguous would be an attempt to crash a highjacked airliner into a nuclear power plant. The speculation about the intended target of the fourth airliner seized on September 11, 2001 (before it crashed as the hostages on board heroically attempted to take back control of the plane) included the Three Mile Island nuclear power plant in Pennsylvania.[6]

Now that the world faces the possibility of cyber warfare, attacks on computer systems by opposing states or by "hacker" terrorist groups, we might experience the destruction of an electric-power-producing nuclear reactor without any physical strike utilizing high explosives, but simply by a very clever penetration of the computerized controls that kept such a reactor running safely.[7] If this were to impose "nuclear damage" on the surrounding countryside and/or impede the production of fissionable materials by the owner of the reactor, the question of whether this had constituted "nuclear escalation" would hardly be so clear.

If there were to be a conventional preemptive attack against existing nuclear weapons on the opposing side, and the attack were somehow to cause one such weapon to explode (perhaps being a primitive design, not as safe against premature detonation as the advanced designs of the United States or Russia), we would also have to debate whether this constituted the violation of the taboo. The Israeli attack on Osirak was clearly not seen as having crossed this line, but an Indian conventional attack on the Pakistani nuclear arsenal might be something different. For a parallel scenario, hardly very much removed from today's news, one could consider a Japanese attempt at a conventional preemption of the North Korean nuclear arsenal, an attempt to eliminate the warheads and missiles involved before Japan itself could be directly threatened.

As yet another more marginal and categorically ambiguous case, it is possible that the "nuclear escalation" would be a desperate move by a state that has not yet perfected its weapons, with the result that we would see a "fizzle," just as one sometimes had experienced in the nuclear weapons test programs of the established nuclear powers, with much less blast and heat than in the attacks of 1945. If the nuclear detonation occurred during a major crisis or in a conventional war that was already well under way but did not inflict damage on the adversary, it could again be debated as to whether it really constituted nuclear escalation in the sense being studied here.

The possibility is always with us that the nuclear warhead used by one of the powers might have an explosive yield much less than what had been desired by its designers, a yield significantly less perhaps than that of the bombs used at Hiroshima and Nagasaki.[8] If such a bomb were to be detonated in an attempt to have an impact on the battlefield, it is even possible that that nuclear escalation would be shrugged off by the adversary, with the world regarding this introduction of nuclear weapons as a futile and ridicule-provoking act of desperation. If the "dud" or "fizzle" in the nuclear warhead were extreme enough, this might thus fall into our ambiguity category, with the best policy for the United States and for the world perhaps then being to act as if the nuclear line had not been crossed, as if the pattern of non-use of nuclear weapons since Nagasaki were still in place.

If such a dud of a bomb were detonated in a city, however, a city as densely populated as those of South Asia, it is hardly plausible that the damage could be shrugged off, for tens of thousands might still be killed, perhaps not quite as many as in the Japanese cities, but still in a comparable magnitude of horror and casualties. Where a city was the chosen target, unless the nuclear warhead was an almost total dud, comparable to the explosive impact of a nuclear "garbage bomb," the result would probably be a total of dead and wounded that the world could not ignore.

An entirely conventional attack could be mistaken for a nuclear attack. The United States and other powers have developed some very large and powerful conventional warheads, intended for destroying the hardened underground bunkers that may house an enemy command post or a hard-shielded weapons system. Such "bunker-buster" bombs radiate a sound signal when they are used and an underground seismic signal that could be mistaken from a distance for the signature of a small nuclear warhead. American "daisy-cutter" weapons of this type were used in the Desert Storm operation[9] and then a decade later in the air attacks on Al Qaeda in Afghanistan, and in each instance some of the listening posts of foreign governments in the region may have concluded initially that the United States *might* have used a nuclear warhead.

Given the inclinations of the press to watch for the most exciting and pessimistic of news events, it would not take very much to produce a leak of such a report and a press declaration that the nuclear taboo had been violated. In this discussion, we will be focusing most on the responses of the *democratic* governments if a nuclear weapon is used. This is in part because any book like this is much more likely to be read in the democracies and because democracy has indeed made great progress since 1989 in how much of the world it governs. Yet, it is important to note that democracy, however desirable it is in preference to alternative systems of government, depends on an unfettered press and thus tends to be burdened by an often irresponsible and sensationalistic press, one that attracts viewers and sells newspapers by finding bad and frightening news.

The democratic world is surely not so gullible as to believe all of what the free press reports, or else people would be fleeing the checkout lines of every supermarket to escape the invasions of aliens from outer space. If a major conventional detonation were thus to be falsely reported as having been a nuclear detonation, most of the world would probably suspend its judgment until the report was confirmed; and the more-educated citizens of such democracies would turn to their more-serious newspapers to see how the ambiguous event was being reported. This avoidance of a rush to pessimistic judgment would also, of course, reflect the fact that nuclear weapons have *indeed not* been used since 1945. The report would be less believable, given this precedent, and there would be a desire not to believe it.

Just as it might be desirable for the democratic governments to keep pessimism from sinking in when the event was *definitionally* marginal, it would be important for them to do the same when the facts were ambiguous, for example, when a large detonation during some ongoing warfare was conventional, not nuclear as it may have seemed. If the facts support the persistence of the "nuclear taboo," it may be in the interest of the democracies to make sure that these facts are clear and widely disseminated.

Related to all the possibilities of ambiguity suggested thus far, one could imagine many cases of *false accusation* of nuclear weapons use, especially where very-small-yield nuclear weapons were known to be an option for one or both sides. If the explosion of a large conventional-weapons storage magazine were to look like a nuclear detonation to an untrained observer, this might lead to the circulation of misleading reports by propaganda agents and by sensationalist news organizations, leaving the world unsure of whether nuclear weapons had actually been used.

One might also encounter unconfirmable accusations that one side had been in the process of launching a nuclear attack, only to be preempted by the opposing side's conventional air strikes or by the effectiveness of its air defenses, which had shot down a plane possibly carrying a nuclear warhead.

Similarly ambiguous as to whether it should be counted as a violation of the nuclear taboo would be the initiation of nuclear testing during an ongoing crisis.[10] While the intent would clearly be to intimidate and shake up the opposing side, most analysts would be quick to say that this does not really amount to a crossing the line. In the past, the Soviets tested massive thermonuclear weapons during periods of tension with the West.[11] However much these increased the general feeling of crisis, as did all the efforts on either side to employ the mere threat of nuclear warfare as a mode of deterrence or pressure on the other, we still remember our history as showing that nuclear weapons have *not* been used in anger since 1945.

Such tests would have come closer to the line if they were conducted in close physical proximity to the opposing side or perhaps high in the air over some disputed territory or over international waters. The Indian test detonations of 1998 were not conducted as far as possible from the Pakistani border but rather in a desert area in the northwest of India, and the Pakistani tests were also not conducted as far as possible from the Indian border.[12] But again, we remember these tests as frustrations of the world's attempt to prevent nuclear weapons proliferation, not as violations of whatever taboo has emerged on nuclear weapons *use*.

Pushing such a marginal case further, a possessor of nuclear weapons might choose to conduct a "test" detonation at the tensest time of some political and military crisis, a detonation which might collapse some mountain pass very close to the line of confrontation or inflict substantial electromagnetic pulse (EMP) effects. Where the nuclear explosion did not directly violate the sovereignty of other countries, as determined by existing boundaries and truce lines, this might be viewed as nothing more than saber-rattling in the traditional ways of publicizing the threats of basic deterrence. But, if the actual detonation came close enough to enemy forces to shake the ground under them or force them to look away from a bright flash of light, we would then again be into a debate on whether nuclear weapons had not actually been "used" rather than merely brandished.

Another ambiguous case, perhaps the hardest to define away, would be the use of a nuclear weapon in a civil war, when a country's nuclear arsenal is used against itself after its armed forces have broken into competing factions. This relates to the breakdowns of command and control that concern us particularly in regard to nuclear terrorism, amounting to a powerful argument for assisting countries with their command-and-control arrangements once they have defied the world's nonproliferation regime and gone ahead and acquired nuclear weapons.

Finally, if a nuclear warhead were to be detonated within its possessor's own territory as the result of a simple accident, would we regard this as a violation of the "nuclear taboo"? Most probably not, even if a substantial number of people were killed by the blast or the radioactive fallout. However, if such a detonation occurred because some officer had gone berserk, would we regard this as a crossing of the line? And what if, instead of a single officer, an entire division of the army had rebelled and elected to detonate such a weapon?

Sooner or later, on this continuum, the world would have to sense that "nuclear war" was under way, even if it remained within the boundaries of what had been a single state. Sooner or later, the situation would not match—and could not be made to match—anyone's common sense that the pattern of global nuclear non-use was still in place.

The line would certainly not be crossed, however, if an internal conflict saw the mere *threat* of a use of nuclear weapons. We have had several real-life examples of such brandishing: in the tumult of the Great Cultural Revolution in Mao's Communist China, where the PLA general in charge of the nuclear facilities in Xinjiang was reported to have warned the Red Guards to stay away from his operation;[13] and, a little earlier, in the French Army coup attempt against de Gaulle in Algeria, where a nuclear device scheduled to be test-detonated in the Saharan Desert was exploded several days early, lest it fall under the control of the rebellious generals.[14]

The *clearest* scenario of escalation is that where a nuclear weapon actually is detonated on a target, with no possibilities of false accusation or rumor and no argument that it might have been only a test intended to intimidate an opponent during a crisis. But our advance planning for a nuclear escalation must be capable of handling the more ambiguous possibilities as well as the very clear-cut.

Cases with Surprisingly Low Collateral Damage (Category B)

To illustrate what frightens most people so much about the prospect of nuclear war, one could sort the categories of attack quantitatively by destructiveness. Will the casualties inflicted in this next use of nuclear weapons be in the tens of thousands, as at Hiroshima and Nagasaki, or in the hundreds of thousands, or in the millions? Or will the casualties instead, because the target was carefully chosen as a military location far away from any civilian population center, be less than a thousand, with almost none of those being civilians? Might there even be no human casualties at all?

The second set of nuclear escalation scenarios comprises definite crossings of the line, but with surprisingly little damage to human life, and with the world's reaction thus being more one of relief, perhaps leading to a willingness to see nuclear weapons as potentially "ordinary" weapons. (To repeat a point made several times, this is *not* the nuclear escalation that we are all the most braced against.)

In this category of nuclear escalation there would be no doubt about whether a nuclear weapon had actually been used, but the world would be pleasantly surprised that little or no collateral damage had been inflicted, that very few or no civilians, or perhaps no people at all, had been killed or wounded. Our normal view of nuclear weapons is that they are weapons of "mass destruction," but if a defensive antimissile system were to utilize a nuclear warhead to intercept and destroy an incoming missile (to cite just one example), there would be no such mass destruction involved.

The weapons laboratories of the established nuclear powers are capable of producing nuclear weapons with very low yields in blast, heat, and radioactivity, such that the smallest of such weapons might do no more collateral damage and no more intended damage than a conventional warhead. The world has not seen any demonstration in real practice that a nuclear weapon could cause less collateral damage than would be suffered in a similar campaign waged entirely with conventional weapons. Given our memories of the scenes of Hiroshima and Nagasaki, this very much contradicts our intuitions. Yet, at least in terms of abstract calculations, the possibility loomed in the Cold War years that, were there a Soviet tank advance into West Germany, it might have been repulsed more effectively, with fewer casualties among German civilians, if tactical nuclear weapons were used than if the attempt to hold back the Soviet advance were conducted entirely with conventional weapons. Some would see this as nothing more than the self-promoting wishful thinking of American nuclear weapons designers,[15] but to reject it out of hand would be to engage in the same closed-minded thinking that underpins any taboo. At the minimum, the world will have to be prepared for an initiation of nuclear war that is surprising for how *little* damage it inflicts, as well as for an initiation that is shocking by how much damage is inflicted.

It can be said with some certainty that the United States and its allies have welcomed the absence of nuclear weapons use since 1945. A tremendous amount of destruction and misery have been avoided, including destruction within the United States itself. Yet, throughout the Cold War, in what sometimes seemed like a logical contradiction, or at least a moral paradox, the United States and its allies had to welcome the *threat* of such nuclear escalation, a threat which hopefully would never have to be executed, a threat which prevented the outbreak of the conventional wars that might otherwise have occurred in central Europe or elsewhere around the world (wars that would not have been nearly as destructive as nuclear war but that would have produced a great deal of misery nonetheless).[16]

While the nuclear taboo partly stems from the fact that these nuclear threats ("the threat that leaves something to chance" in Thomas Schelling's phrase[17]) never had to be executed, the deterrent power of the threat has also been eroded by the taboo, as the world more and more came to regard nuclear escalation, the backbone of "extended nuclear deterrence," as unthinkable. This erosion has been a source of concern for U.S. military strategists.

With the collapse of the Warsaw Pact and of the Soviet Union itself, the argument is often made that the United States, and its allies in NATO and South Korea and elsewhere, no longer have any need for extended nuclear deterrence.[18] Since the United States is now manifestly superior to every possible adversary in terms of conventional military capability, perhaps it should welcome the nuclear taboo, rather than regarding it as a dangerous impediment to the credibility of nuclear escalation threats.

Yet scenarios remain wherein the United States, and indeed several of its allies, will want to maintain the credibility of American nuclear escalation.[19] The outcomes of conventional wars are always difficult to predict, even when one side has pronouncedly better weapons; and over the next two or three decades, other countries may find ways to overcome the American conventional-weaponry advantage. And opposing powers, even if totally unable to cope with American conventional capabilities, may have chemical and biological options that they are tempted to employ. The threat of an American introduction of nuclear weapons will thus remain relevant, as a response to a surprising conventional breakthrough by an adversary and as a deterrent to such an adversary's attack on the United States homeland or its forces with *other* weapons of mass destruction.

While the priorities of choice have indeed shifted, the paradoxical balance remains in place. The United States and the other liberal democracies in the world will welcome every year that goes by without the use of nuclear weapons, but they will at the same time want to retain the plausible threat that such weapons could be used *under some circumstances* and hope that the *threat* will be sufficient to prevent the circumstances. Success on either half of this balance undermines the other half. This was true during the Cold War, and it will remain true for the foreseeable future.

In addition to perhaps being necessary as a hypothetical deterrent response to someone else's use of chemical and biological weapons (CBW), nuclear weapons could come into a very benign use if they were to be the only means of digging out and decisively destroying someone's stockpile of very deadly weapons. It is sometimes conjectured that, if biological or chemical agents were buried underground in a bunker, a conventional attack on the bunker would be too likely to release the deadly materials, inflicting great damage to anyone downwind. A nuclear explosion detonated after penetration into the bunker might be the only means to burn away and destroy all the deadly CBW material, and one would thus have another example in which use of nuclear weapons had saved lives rather than taking lives.

To repeat, any case in which a use of nuclear weapons kills very few or no people, where it indeed saves the lives of a significant number of people, would be much less likely to draw condemnation around the world. But its implications for the future of other uses of nuclear weapons, for the maintenance of any more-categorical nuclear taboo, will be very troublesome.

There are a great many ways in which nuclear weapons use would amount to a disaster for the world (most readers might regard this as the most obvious statement in the world). Yet there are some uses of nuclear weapons that would not amount to a disaster, that actually would solve problems rather than exacerbate them. One of our greatest difficulties for the future might be that the *precedent* set by such a relatively benign use of nuclear weapons would make it more difficult thereafter to head off all the uses that would create disaster and holocaust.

If a major conventional war had been under way for an extended period of time, as for example the prolonged Iran-Iraq conflict of the 1980s, a sudden introduction of nuclear weapons into such a war might bring it just as suddenly to an end; and the world, rather than reacting with shock and dismay, might heave a sigh of relief. (The destructions of Hiroshima and Nagasaki were received as good news by many in East Asia and around the world, since World War II would thus quickly be terminated.) All horror is relative to what the situation was before the horrific event. A nuclear attack "out of the blue" would cause much more shock than a nuclear attack during a war which had already killed tens of thousands of people.

Very dangerous as a precedent, therefore, might be some of the benign introductions of nuclear weapons suggested above—where a defensive missile uses a nuclear warhead to stop an incoming missile carrying a biological warhead, or where a nuclear depth charge is used to destroy an adversary's submarine, or where a deep-penetrating nuclear warhead is used to kill off the leaders of a terrorist organization hiding in an underground shelter.

Advocates of such "battlefield" uses of nuclear weapons could, in all fairness, note that there is nothing really immoral or bad about the low-collateral-damage arsenal they have assembled. Yet, setting good precedents in this, without setting bad precedents in the process, will be a very difficult task indeed. As Thomas Schelling noted almost a half-century ago, much of the restraint of limited war and mutual deterrence has been based on the distinctions people have drawn in their minds between seemingly clear categories, with "nuclear" versus "conventional" being one of the most important of such distinctions.[20]

The line between "low-collateral-damage" and "high-collateral-damage" weapons is much less clear, by contrast, much less usable as a distinction of mutual restraint.

As noted, the use of nuclear weapons can always be primarily countervalue in intent, directed to kill a large number of people by striking at a city. But it might, conversely, be truly planned and executed to minimize such damage, aiming instead to serve some basically military purpose, in what could broadly be labeled a counterforce mode of attack. Indeed, an adversary might be extremely subtle and clever, designing the nuclear attack to inflict very little damage on the United States, with the implicit message that heftier kinds of retaliation were being held in reserve, in case the United States or another power reacted too much to this first nuclear use.

Such an attempt to impose a minimum of collateral damage on civilian targets might be based on moral feelings or on a desire to avoid alienating world opinion or offending the moral sensibilities of other states, as well as on a carefully calculated scheme of holding layers of destructiveness in reserve, in a strategy of limited nuclear war and graduated deterrence.

Yet another important motive might be the aggressor's desire to preserve intact the objective of its aggression. A prime example of this would be the likely approach of Beijing toward Taiwan if the Chinese Communists decided to take military action to gain control over the island and then elected to include nuclear weapons in the action. In addition to having to offer the United States a reason to withhold the maximum of retaliation it could inflict on China, Beijing would be taking world opinion into account, of course, hoping to manipulate this opinion in its own favor; but it would most importantly desire to avoid destroying the very province whose people and economic assets it was so much seeking to govern.[21]

Such an event of minimal-countervalue nuclear escalation might also quite easily be the action of a power friendly to the United States, or of the United States itself. The hypothetical NATO nuclear escalations of the Cold War, designed (apparently *successfully*) to deter conventional or other initiatives by the Warsaw Pact, supply a host of models for how this form of nuclear escalation could occur in the future.

At the extreme of low-collateral-damage nuclear escalation are the possibilities of totally nonlethal violations of the nuclear taboo, perhaps use of nuclear warheads as part of a missile defense system that stops an incoming missile from striking a city, in the process saving tens of thousands of lives while taking none; or perhaps a nuclear detonation utilized for EMP effects, to interfere with the electronic communications of an adversary.

It is even possible that a use of nuclear weapons somewhere would be driven primarily by someone's desire to erase the nuclear taboo: someone could be seeking to get the world accustomed to the idea that the use of such weapons might be thinkable and morally acceptable in the future. To "break the ice," it would be very appropriate to find a use of nuclear weapons that saved lives rather than taking them and that seemed morally very just, rather than a punishment of the innocent.

If Israel were thus to employ a nuclear warhead on a TMD (theater missile defense) missile to destroy an incoming Iranian warhead thought to be carrying chemical or biological weapons, it would be *only* Israel that had violated the *nuclear* taboo, but world opinion might well applaud the action nonetheless. One might sense similar applause rather than condemnation if the nuclear warhead were part of a counter-bunker or counter-cave missile attack designed to punish and eliminate some particularly obnoxious dictator or an instigator of terrorism like Osama bin Laden. If nuclear ASW (antisubmarine warfare) weapons were to be used to destroy an enemy submarine that one had been trying and failing to destroy with conventional depth charges, there would presumably be *no* civilian collateral damage, as the target being destroyed would be totally military.

Irresponsible Nuclear Escalations (Category C)

One of the most worrisome aspects of the September 11th attack is that it dispelled any presumption that terrorists inherently limited the amount of destruction they would want to inflict, and therefore the presumption that terrorists would not utilize nuclear warheads if they were ever able to lay their hands on them.[22]

In the third category of scenarios there would be no doubts about whether nuclear weapons had been used, and degree of collateral damage would not be an issue; but there would instead be uncertainties about who had launched such an attack and whether any state regime was in charge of the nuclear forces that had been used.[23]

Aside from the natural concern now about the terrorists, who may be "irresponsible" and "undeterrable" as compared with normal state regimes, one always has to worry about breakdowns of state command and control in any war that is under way. If the heat of combat and fog of war make it difficult for heads of government to reach their field commanders, these commanders may launch nuclear attacks that would not have been authorized.

Concerns about terrorist motivation and about loss of normal command and control blend together to produce a compounded problem of responsibility. As we sort the kinds of possible target for any nuclear escalation, one choice has always pertained to whether the attack would be intended to eliminate the victim's command-and-control system or was instead directed and limited so as to maintain an extensive capacity for post-strike communications and bargaining, and thus perhaps war termination. In the former case, the capital city of the victim might be a prime target, while in the latter the capital city would be spared.[24]

Governments would, under many circumstances, have a strong incentive to preserve their adversary's ability to negotiate and to surrender; terrorists, by contrast, might have a much stronger incentive to create general chaos, to disrupt and destroy all of their target's ability to control and moderate its responses. A nuclear exchange in the days of the Cold War might have seen Moscow electing to keep Washington functioning, and vice versa.[25] To the extent that a terrorist use of nuclear weapons rises higher on a U.S. list of probabilities to be feared, the peril rises of an attack on Washington, D.C., as terrorists would have little vested interest in maintaining a functioning American government.

Terrorists may not only be irresponsible by the standards of normal governments; they may have an interest in making normal governments irresponsible as well.

This third category comprises the scenarios where the use of nuclear weapons is damaging but may have been accidental or insubordinate, such that the anger at the government whose weapons had been detonated might be tempered by some sympathy. These would thus be cases where the immediate follow-on to a nuclear escalation might not be an atmosphere of urgent reaction but rather of broad confusion about what was to be done and about how urgently it needed to be done. The state whose weapons were used might itself be very remorseful about the attack, rendering the target government far less clear about whether punishment and retaliation were in order. The situation might be more than a little analogous to the confusions we feel about the "insanity defense" in cases of homicide.

We are already relatively ready to think about a case in which India and Pakistan, in a set of national government decisions, used nuclear weapons against each other; but there are South Asian scenarios in which the identity of those making the decisions would be much less certain. Pakistan is a state which could break into pieces while continuing to possess nuclear weapons[26] (the Soviet Union was, of course, the clear example of the same concerns in 1991[27]); what happens to such weapons in the chaos of the breakup would set the stage for several "first use since Nagasaki" possibilities.

Given the large number of nuclear weapons that were produced during the Cold War, the inherent risk confronts us that nuclear weapons could come into the possession of terrorists or even ordinary criminals, whose use of such warheads would be very different from that characteristic of a state. At the most elementary level, the appropriate retaliation for such a first use of nuclear weapons since 1945 would be much less clear, since the perpetrators would hold no territory and have no cities against which retaliatory threats could be directed.

We have, all through the Cold War, lived with the risks of unauthorized firings of nuclear missiles and other such introductions of nuclear weapons by insubordinate officers within established state militaries.[28] Indeed, one of the more important arguments in favor of national missile defense (NMD) antimissile systems has been this unignorable possibility.

The officers launching such an attack might be sufficiently abnormal in their psychology that common sense would label them "crazy." Indeed even elected or otherwise duly constituted heads of government might fall into this category; they might be "crazy" in the sense of being undeterrable, of being indifferent to the retaliation that has thus far accounted for the non-use of nuclear weapons since 1945.

At one step away from the concern about a possibly crazy insubordinate military officer, we would have to include on our list a totally accidental detonation of a nuclear weapon. If the accident merely devastated its own base, most of us would hardly regard this as nuclear escalation or as a breaking of the "nuclear taboo." If the accident instead involved a missile's traveling to destroy the target at which it had been aimed for all these years, that would be much more what we are concerned about here, and one part of the problem would, of course, be demonstrating or proving that it had indeed been "an accident."

If the source of an attack were much more diffuse than our normal model of a state regime, the likely reactions of the world, and our ideal reactions as a matter of policy analysis, would change. A suggestive model is thrust upon us, obviously, by the events of September 11, 2001, which relied on the willingness of the immediate perpetrators to commit suicide in the execution of the attack, hence converging on what we normally regard as "undeterrable."

The very understandable response, in the case of the World Trade Center attacks, has been to assume that one state or another in the outside world must bear *some* responsibility for the attack, if only for having housed and based the perpetrators and having tolerated their actions. Elementary logic suggests that harboring such perpetrators is inconsistent with the safety of the world. If one gives up on finding any motivational lever to deter suicidal attackers, one might nonetheless at least be able, by imposing punishment, to deter any *governments* from serving in the future as such helpful hosts for such terrorists.[29]

Any state supporting a nuclear terrorist attack would almost surely have a nonsuicidal, this-world interest in retaining political power, in remaining the government of a state. As in the case of the Taliban in Afghanistan, it is thus an appropriate target for retaliation, to restore the expectations required for deterrence. Even if the perpetrators of the attack commit suicide or otherwise disappear from the scene without being noticeably punished, their host government will suffer the tangible punishment of being deposed from power.

But if no such state support were required for a nuclear attack, the world response, and American response, would have to shift to searching for other important motives to influence.

In summation, it may not be certain that *all* terrorism has to be "state-sponsored," that is, that every terrorist group has to get the support of at least one actual state, if only to maintain a home base and headquarters. Ordinary terrorism and some future non-state uses of nuclear weapons might be carried off without the approval or knowledge of *any* existing state. If so, we will be without a geographic target for retaliation, an important vehicle for deterrence.

There will be an urgent need to find *some* appropriate form of retaliation against attackers like those involved in the events of September 11, but this might thus pose a temptation to come up with a state supporter, whether or not there really is one.

Given how horrible most forms of nuclear war would be, it may indeed be more likely that any such escalation would come in *this* form, which in turn implies a greater risk of attack on Washington, D.C., and other national capitals.

Even before the September 11th suicide attacks on New York and Washington, the world had been debating the conceptual and definitional issues of whether terrorists might be "rational" or not. If someone has been told and believes that his own death in the service of a religious cause will lead him to a very pleasant version of the afterlife, one could hardly describe this as "irrational," as an example of someone not relating means to ends in a calculated way.

The issue of "rationality" was debated all through the Cold War by critics of a reliance on mutual deterrence.[30] "Deterrence presupposes rationality" was a phrase that could be seized upon by the psychologists and other social scientists who were opposed to nuclear weapons, as they responded that their clinical experience showed that almost no one was fully rational. No one considers every aspect of a choice, and no one has personal goals and preferences that are entirely free of neurosis.

But a much less stringent test than this may have been required to establish rationality. The concept of rationality relates to both the information that an individual possesses and the normality or abnormality of his or her preferences. One can illustrate this with two homely examples, relating to the ability to fly and the ability to do murder.

How many of us believe that we are capable of flying like a bird? Almost no one believes this, unless they have been consuming LSD. Anyone who has such an erroneous impression of the facts is indeed mentally ill, unable to process one of the most basic facts of human life. How many of us would like to fly like a bird? Almost everyone, for the shortening of our commutes, for the pleasure of seeing the countryside. There would be nothing mentally ill or "irrational" in our cravings here.

How many of us believe that we are capable of killing people? Any intelligent person knows that if we ran our automobile into a line of people waiting at a bus stop, at least some of them would most likely die. There is nothing irrational about being aware of this ability to kill (indeed, this awareness could make us more careful as we drive home). How many of us would *want* to kill people? Almost no one, and such a preference would indeed strike most of us as "sick," "psychotic," or "irrational." These two cases illustrate how when we question rationality we may at one time be addressing the information that individuals handle and at another time may be addressing their preferences.

Returning to nuclear deterrence, the "rationality" that was required for deterrence to work was therefore far less than having totally reliable information or a set of preferences totally free of neuroses and abnormalities. What was needed for effective deterrence between Moscow and Washington was simply that the decision makers in both capitals be, in terms of *information,* aware of the elementary logical linkage by which a nuclear attack against the other power would produce a nuclear retaliation, and that they additionally be, in terms of *preferences,* averse to that retaliation.

These were relatively simple requirements to fulfill. The risks were very low (never zero) that a leader in either country would be so muddle-headed as not to understand the elementary deterrence mechanism ("they won't as long as I don't, but they will if I do"), or that he or she would be so uninterested in the physical survival of their cities as not to mind nuclear retaliation.

The problem becomes much more severe if nuclear or other weapons of mass destruction fall into the control of individuals who do not control cities or who do not mind the destruction of the cities they do control, perhaps because (as a "rogue state" about to be subjected to a "regime change") they are slated to be deposed and thus have "nothing left to lose," or perhaps because their calculations about the attractiveness of the afterlife render the cities and structure of this life unimportant.

The risks of anonymous or unattributable nuclear attacks are worsened, of course, by the possibility that nuclear weapons might be stolen from an existing arsenal; the nuclear weapons of the former Soviet Union have been a prime subject of such concerns ever since 1990.[31] Rather than having to deal with a primitive atomic bomb slapped together by a rogue state or a terrorist group, the world would have to confront a very modern design, easily portable, with a relatively high explosive yield, perhaps even a "suitcase bomb" that could be delivered by truck.[32] And the "nuclear fingerprint" of the isotopes released would not tell the outside world much about who had been the perpetrator of the nuclear attack, only what the original source of the weapon had been.

Somewhere in between is the scenario in which the bomb is not stolen from an arsenal but is also not the crude product of inexperienced weapons designers in some non-nuclear state or terrorist group. Rather, it is produced by unemployed weapons designers from the former Soviet Union or from any other country that has already been producing such weapons.[33] Individuals with nuclear-weapons-design competence might also be driven by greed, even if they are not made desperate by unemployment. And, just as such material greed has sometimes caused Americans to engage in espionage for the Soviet Union, shocking their fellow Americans when the crime was uncovered, it is not beyond imagination that an alumnus of the weapons laboratories of the United States could be the guilty party in providing a nuclear warhead to an irresponsible group or state.

If a nuclear explosion occurs somewhere in the world, with no one claiming credit for the attack and with no immediate war or crisis nearby to give a hint as to the motivation, the impact for the world's attitudes and for appropriate policy responses will hardly be clear. Even today, one periodically sees attacks on the public that are simply the initiative of an individual who is insane by any definition, and that reflect no political cause or national agenda.

Where such an act of simple irrationality did not reflect any broader cause, the world might shrug it off as not a violation of the taboo, maintaining the feeling that nuclear weapons are not "just another weapon." The sheer horror of what had happened might indeed even reinforce the nuclear taboo, rather than being seen as erasing it. (To turn to a grisly parallel, occasionally someone who is insane engages in cannibalism; when such an act is discovered, the world does not become more willing to consider cannibalism as an alternative to be chosen by ordinary people.)

If the anonymous nuclear attack could more likely be connected to a political agenda, however, there would be a greater risk that new patterns of international behavior would thereafter set in. Even without any particular actor's coming forward to claim credit for a nuclear explosion, the world would guess, if the destroyed city were in some country already embroiled in international disputes, that there was nonetheless a political motive behind the attack.

Ever since the attacks of September 11th, the world has been focused, perhaps excessively, on the risks of *Islamic* terrorism, involving a willingness to commit suicide, as part of making certain that the terrorist attack inflicts a large enough number of homicides. A cautionary note must be that it would be oversimplifying Islam to lump all of it together as prone to engaging in terrorism and as fanatic to the point of suicide. And the concomitant to this note would be that there have been *other* forces in history that were also ready to commit suicide, the Japanese Kamikaze attacks in World War II being a major example, and more recently the suicidal Tamil Tigers.[34] Would Tamil terrorists, or the Sikh terrorists who destroyed several airliners, killing all on board, or the contemporary Japanese terrorists who launched a poison gas attack on the Tokyo subway not be willing to launch a nuclear attack? And there may be still other factions, perhaps motivated by nothing more than material considerations and simple greed, like the Revolutionary Armed Forces of Colombia or the drug cartels in Colombia, or the pirates now plaguing the Malacca Strait, that would be willing to exploit a nuclear weapon if they could acquire one, and willing to detonate such a weapon to destroy an entire city as a way to win their demands.

The world's problems with responding to such substate terrorism, if it ever reaches the nuclear level, will be everywhere severe, since it will be difficult to determine who bore the actual responsibility for the attack and whom one should retaliate against.

One of the possibilities of an insubordinate use of nuclear weapons cited above would be in a *nuclear* civil war, wherein the nuclear weapons of country X were used against a city within country X or against other military forces inside country X. Since no international boundary was crossed in this version of nuclear escalation, some analysts might question whether this was actually a resumption of what had ended at Nagasaki; but the common sense of most of us would be that nuclear weapons had indeed been *used* intentionally and that the nuclear taboo had indeed been broken.

The Chinese and French examples from the 1960s illustrate only the *brandishing* of nuclear weapons, the deterring possibilities of punishment that always attach to the existence of nuclear weapons, in a domestic and internal equivalent of what has indeed been normal practice in the international sphere ever since nuclear weapons were introduced. Nuclear weapons have been "*used*" over and over again as a deterrent since Nagasaki, sometimes within countries.

Nuclear weapons have *not* been used in actual detonations against a hostile target during these years, internationally or domestically. If such a use comes now, be it a city that is destroyed or a military target, one possibility will be that the weapon will have been one of its own country's nuclear warheads. If civil war in Spain brought about the bombardment of Barcelona, a civil war in the twenty-first century might produce a *nuclear* bombardment of some city.

Reactions to Mass Destruction: Preemptive Surrender? (Category D)

The remaining categories of possible nuclear escalation would remove all the qualifications introduced thus far. There would not, as in Category A, be any doubt about whether this was a definite use of nuclear weapons. There would not, as in Category B, emerge any surprisingly good news of low collateral damage, with few or no civilians being killed. And there would not, as in Category C, be any question about whether a *state* was responsible for the nuclear attack. Rather, we would have what all of us normally expect and dread as the prospect of the next use of nuclear weapons, a definite and deliberate use of nuclear weapons in a way that inflicted great damage.

Because a nuclear attack on a city, amid expectations of more such attacks to come, is the scenario that we all dread the most, it is also a scenario which could produce very substantial intimidation around the world; the perpetrator of such an attack, rather than being confronted and resisted, might instead get his way. The goal for anyone acquiring nuclear weapons (and then threatening to use them, or actually using them) has all along been to instill and exploit such intimidation; this, after all, is what nuclear deterrence is all about.

In our fourth category of scenarios, a very worrisome reaction might thus show up in some countries (and even in some portions of American opinion), that whoever had been willing to launch such a nuclear attack now had to be appeased, that any demands made for withdrawal from various foreign positions should be granted, that the appropriate response, when a repetition of such massive destruction was being threatened, would be a form of surrender.[35] In the service of the American national interest and the world's interests, some major thought must be given to how such a defeatist response to nuclear escalation can be headed off.

The nuclear attack we are contemplating here could come tomorrow, even as this analysis is being read. Yet, if a longer period of time elapses before such an event, the offensive and defensive weapons at hand will have changed, and this evolution of available weapons may also affect how the world reacts, and how the United States ideally *should* react. The United States may itself have acquired a national missile defense system in this interval, and such protection may have been deployed to protect Western Europe or Japan.[36] If a nuclear attack is blunted by such a defense—perhaps a primitive nuclear warhead on a rudimentary missile is destroyed or is diverted so that no serious damage is done—very different reactions may emerge, as compared to the straight-out destruction of a city or an airbase.

But the reliability of such missile defense may always be in some doubt. Different responses would apply if the missile defenses turned out to be ineffective, such that it would not be the nuclear escalation that seemed physically foolish but the futile attempt to defend against it.

If the first nuclear attack is not directed at the United States but at a third party, it thus will be important, in assessing likely and ideal American reactions, to know whether or not the United States has in the meantime acquired a degree of NMD protection plausibly sufficient to be effective against the attacker. If the first user of nuclear weapons were Russia, or China, we might presume that the United States would *not* have acquired this degree of protection.[37]

The delivery means exploited in the initial nuclear escalation will affect the reactions. If the nuclear warhead were delivered by a standard weapons delivery system, for example, a bomber or a missile, the responses might be very different than if such a warhead had been brought to its target by a tramp steamer or by a drug-runner DC-6. The reaction to the latter kind of attack might be that it would be bluntable, once we were aware of the risk; but the reaction to standard bomber or missile attack (especially where no air or missile defenses had seemed robust enough to repulse the attacks) would be much less to count on enhanced defenses.

Also important in sorting out the reactions is if the attack has occurred after extensive nuclear proliferation, whether many more than ten countries possess such weapons or there has been a more contained degree of nuclear weapons spread. Similarly important will be the degree of other WMD proliferation. The world will react with less shock to a nuclear escalation if numerous biological and chemical WMD attacks have already been perpetrated on civilian or military targets.

When a country like Israel or North Korea today moves to acquire nuclear weapons and in the process reinsures its own continued existence, despite the hostility and disapproval of its neighbors, one could read even this as the world's giving in to the fear of nuclear destruction. But, as long as such basic deterrence works without the weapons' actually having to be detonated, we do not have the violation of the nuclear taboo we are contemplating throughout this book; we instead have only a continuation of the nuclear deterrence by threat that has been the pattern for all the years since Nagasaki, as has been so aptly analyzed by Pierre Gallois,[38] Kenneth Waltz,[39] and many others.

Rather than speculating about the aftermath of any new *use* of nuclear weapons, many analysts today see the most pressing and relevant topic to be the aftermath of continued *proliferation* of such weapons. This author's relative optimism about the possibility of avoiding an actual use might indeed be consistent with this focus.

If nuclear weapons spread to more countries, this does not have to mean that they will therefore come into the possession of *every* country. Too extensive a proliferation might indeed raise the likelihoods very high that, somewhere, nuclear weapons will indeed be used. The barrier against proliferation set by the nuclear Non-Proliferation Treaty (NPT) has indeed been cracked (and the "taboo" on nuclear proliferation broken), by the Indian and Pakistani detonations and by Israel's earlier behavior; but this does not mean that the world has renounced the view that nuclear weapons are different from other weapons, such that most countries are better off forgoing their possession (as long as their neighbors do so as well).

The United States in the future may have to consider accepting a *partial* relaxation of its opposition to nuclear proliferation, whereby some additional possessors of such weapons (perhaps Japan, perhaps Saudi Arabia?) would be tolerated, and others not. The expanded possession of such weapons can still work as a deterrent against their use, as it has since 1945. If North Korean or Iranian nuclear weapons provoked some matching proliferation but otherwise settled into a pattern of deterrence, we could perhaps adjust to this. But, if such weapons were actually to be detonated on an opposing city, and if the rest of the world decided as a result to back away even more from confronting the state that had used them, we would have a much more worrisome situation.

Less Defeatist Responses to a Rogue State Attack (Category E)

Our fifth category is situations in which the world reaction, instead of being one of craven retreat, is that punitive action must urgently be taken, that revenge must be inflicted, that the perpetrator must be punished and disabled from committing any such atrocity again.[40]

If a novice possessor of nuclear weapons showed its "immaturity" by using the weapons very quickly after acquiring them, such a regime would not inspire trust about its restraint thereafter and would thus seem to require a punitive intervention. Such a rogue state would, of course, also not be likely to possess any substantial reserve of nuclear weapons with which it could retaliate against any such punitive intervention.

The earliest 1960s speculation about nuclear weapons being acquired by Communist China voiced the kinds of concerns we feel today about irresponsible behavior by a "rogue state." Beijing was then seen as being much more revolutionary and anti-Western than Moscow, and as perhaps ready to use nuclear weapons even when the Soviet leadership would have been deterred. Mao issued some statements (when the Chinese as yet did not have any such weapons) indicating that China would welcome nuclear war, because it had such a large reserve of population.[41] The fanatical Chinese Communists were thus seen as much more likely than any other state to initiate the use of nuclear weapons, or at least to push crises to the brink of such use.

Among the scenarios of concern in this category were the possibilities of a "catalytic" use of a rudimentary nuclear stockpile, wherein the Chinese Communists might have openly destroyed one American city, merely to provoke the United States into a full retaliatory strike against the Soviet Union, which would then produce full Soviet retaliation in return, with substantial damage to the United States, the entire prospect perhaps being sufficient to force the United States to back off if confronted by Beijing. During the 1960s there was speculation along such lines about the role of the *French* nuclear force, sufficient to do enough damage to Moscow to trigger the major exchanges of a World War III, the possibility of which had much more deterrent effect than the destruction it could inflict by itself.[42]

A slightly different version of a Chinese catalytic action had the Chinese bomb destroying some city *without* attribution, in the expectation that Moscow or Washington would be blamed for the attack, provoking world anger and retaliation. One important, if probably imperfect, antidote to this possibility emerged in the American capability for sorting and identifying the signatures of different types of nuclear weapons, based on the monitoring of the first weapons tests, such that a Chinese bomb would not be mistaken for a Soviet bomb.

The world's earlier speculation about Chinese irresponsibility might be relevant in several different ways to our concerns about "rogue states" four decades later. Some more optimistic analysts point to the relative moderation of the Chinese position after Beijing's acquisition of the bomb, and after the death of Mao—its adoption of a policy of no-first-use of nuclear weapons, its adherence to the nuclear Non-Proliferation Treaty, the very slow pace of its nuclear buildup—with the hopeful speculation that other acquirers of nuclear weapons, Pakistan or North Korea or Iran, will also become more moderate once they are actual members of "the club."[43]

Yet few would see such moderation as *guaranteed* in the aftermath of proliferation, and our worry list will inevitably have to include the possibility of irresponsible nuclear weapons use by a nuclear novice, of someone perhaps detonating a bomb with the hope of having an established nuclear power blamed for the attack. More intensive research is thus probably called for in the techniques of identifying nuclear weapons by the isotopes released when they are exploded, lest some country's nuclear weapon be detonated with the intention of casting blame on France or Israel or the United States.

The Communist regime in North Korea has obviously been one of the less rational regimes around the world. The end of the Cold War terminated most of Moscow's influence over Pyongyang. Engaging in terrorist attacks on South Korean leaders and having its midget submarines land agents on South Korean shores, the Pyongyang regime has often seemed to be defeating its own purposes, even while its population is threatened by famine and the world sees its extreme Stalinist version of communism as something very much due to be terminated.[44]

When a government has behaved as unpredictably and seemingly irrationally as that in Pyongyang, other states dread what would happen if that regime possessed weapons of mass destruction and the means to deliver them. Many of the recently discussed scenarios of a future use of nuclear weapons have thus focused on North Korea and the possibility that it would launch a nuclear attack on South Korea, perhaps against Seoul or another city in the ROK, or against military bases in the South, or against Japan or Okinawa or Guam, or (as North Korean missile capabilities are enhanced) against portions of the United States. Given the strangeness of Pyongyang's decision-making processes, one cannot even rule out an attack on Russia or China, Pyongyang's only allies in the recent past. Interestingly, Russia and China are among the countries that are quite unenthusiastic about North Korea's possessing nuclear weapons.

Yet, acquiring and brandishing nuclear weapons could very well serve some quite rational purposes of Kim Jong-il and his regime, working as insurance against the regime's being overturned by a South Korean invasion or by a popular revolution.[45]

In earlier decades, it was South Korea that worried about its viability as a state. The phrase "pariah state" was minted in the 1970s to refer to any regime that was militarily threatened by hostile neighbors while the outside world was inclined to question its overall legitimacy and inclined to look away if a military invasion occurred.[46] The states falling into the "pariah" category included Taiwan, South Africa, Israel, and South Korea, each of which was tempted to get its hands on nuclear weapons, as the only insurance they could find for their existence.

When the world saw Communist forces merge South Vietnam with the Communist North in 1975, there were leftists around the world predicting that the next such "national reunification" would see South Korea eliminated, as yet another puppet regime that had been created and propped up by the United States. President Jimmy Carter then came into office, raising the possibility that American forces would be removed from South Korea. One South Korean response to all this was to move closer to nuclear weapons by exploring plutonium reprocessing, with the result that heavy American pressure was brought to bear on Seoul to terminate such efforts, and also the result that American forces were *not* withdrawn from the ROK.[47]

With the dramatic defeat of communism in the collapse of the Warsaw Pact and of the Soviet Union, the tables were turned, so that it was Pyongyang rather than Seoul that seemed to be the "pariah state," with the forces of history undercutting its legitimacy or continued existence. Rumors of North Korea's violating its commitments under the nuclear Non-Proliferation Treaty then began to emerge.

If the Pyongyang regime plays its cards sensibly and well, therefore, the world will not see its nuclear weapons being used against Japan or South Korea or anyone else, but will rather see this new nuclear arsenal held in reserve (just as the putative Israeli nuclear arsenal has been held in reserve), as a deterrent against the outside world's applying maximal pressure on Pyongyang and as a bargaining chip to extract the economic and political concessions that the DPRK needs if it wishes to avoid giving up its peculiar approach to social engineering. In such a case, North Korea's developing nuclear weapons would not generate any scenarios relevant to the topic of this book but would be one more illustration of the success of the long-running saga of mutual nuclear deterrence. A *very clever* use of North Korean nuclear potential would see no use of weapons, except to extract a more accommodating political attitude from the Americans and Japanese, and from the Chinese, Russians, South Koreans, and everyone else.

But will Pyongyang always be so very clever? The capriciousness of North Korea's actual behavior, under the current North Korean leader and under the leadership of his father, leaves the world with great concerns about *actual use*, rather than the mere exploitation of the shadow of possible use. Every speculation during and since the Cold War about "deterrence failures" has included the risks of leaders' being less than rational, by the normal standards of rationality, and North Korea is a prime example.

Two-Sided Nuclear Wars (Category F)

There might be a comparable urgency but somewhat different guidelines for appropriate interventionary goals if the nuclear escalation was between *two* nuclear weapons countries, each employing these weapons of mass destruction.

This sixth category involves the world's reactions and appropriate policy responses in situations where two states possessing nuclear arsenals have initiated and are continuing nuclear attacks on each other. (One obviously thinks of today's India and Pakistan, but the next three or four decades might see the emergence of other dyads of hostile nuclear states.) The urgency in such cases, where cities are being destroyed each day in the back-and-forth of the attacks, might relate less to punishing and disarming an aggressor and more to terminating the war as quickly as possible.

Some analysts would argue that, by the logic of mutual deterrence, the likelihood of nuclear escalation is less when both sides in a confrontation possess such weapons (as is the case now between Pakistan and India).[48] Others would anticipate a greater risk here than in a crisis or a war between a nuclear power and a non-nuclear-weapons state (as in the conflict between Britain and Argentina).

In the former case, the obvious question is whether one side's use of nuclear weapons would be followed immediately by nuclear retaliation, with the likelihood of much greater totals of casualties, each side being unwilling to be the first to stop the nuclear exchange and perhaps being intent on destroying the remaining nuclear forces of the other side. In the latter case, where the victim has no *nuclear* means of retaliation, there might be a greater chance of a single-shot limited escalation, with the biggest question perhaps pertaining to what the *outside world* would do in response.

If higher ranges of casualties were inflicted, the damage might quickly exhaust the capabilities of the outside world to supply medical and other forms of humanitarian assistance. This would be an exercise in anticipating the more immediate aftermath rather than the longer-term consequences; but, in terms of simple economics and pressures for migration, in many scenarios of use of nuclear weapons, the damage inflicted would be quite severe over even a short range of time.

As noted in Category B above, some uses of nuclear weapons would inflict less damage on the outside world's economy and induce less movement of people as refugees, but nuclear weapons are generally expected to be of great destructive impact. Targets immediately important to the economic functioning of the outside world might be hit, the most striking example being oil refineries or natural gas pipelines. The destruction of virtually any city in the world, given the evolution of global economic interdependence, would adversely affect trading partners everywhere else. If the nuclear escalation occurred during a time of general economic prosperity, the news of the escalation could be expected to slow economies everywhere. If it came at a time of recession, the bad news would worsen conditions.

Moreover, the horror of any attacks on cities and the suffering of the survivors must be expected to drive larger numbers of people to behave just as refugees from poverty behave today, risking their lives on boats manned by unscrupulous smugglers, taxing the energies of immigration authorities everywhere in the developed world.

And, above all, the most likely version of a two-sided nuclear exchange sees a tremendous number of people being killed and wounded, with the wounded desperately needing whatever relief support the outside world can supply.

The Use of Established Nuclear Arsenals (Category G)

There is yet another version of clear and blatant nuclear escalation scenario to which response would be required, from which the world could not simply shrink away, but in which the proper response might be even less clear than in the cases of a rogue-state nuclear novice or of two minor nuclear powers directing their arsenals at each other. We must, as our seventh category, address the possibility that an established nuclear power, one of the states for the moment allowed to retain their nuclear weapons by the terms of the NPT, would do what it did not do for all the Cold War, actually detonate such a weapon "in anger" rather than just in a test, to destroy a city in another country.

In this final category, because the nuclear escalation is launched by a state known to possess a larger arsenal of nuclear weapons, calls are less likely to be voiced for urgent action, for total punishment and "unconditional surrender," as all will be mindful of the inherent constraints of "limited nuclear warfare" and will take into account the enormous destruction that the adversary can still inflict, and has not yet inflicted.

If Russia or China were to take such an initiative, or for that matter, the United States, Britain, or France, this would at least not be a scenario that has never been speculated about. The years of the Cold War indeed saw some extensive speculation on the possibilities of "limited nuclear war," of situations in which one nuclear power or another had made a limited use of its nuclear arsenal while maintaining a hefty force of nuclear weapons in reserve. The other nuclear weapons states, and all the rest of the world, would have to debate how to respond.[49]

Because the first five possessors of nuclear weapons have *not* used them since 1945, even while they have *acquired* a great many of such weapons, one might optimistically project that this restraint will continue, so that this category may be the *least* likely to confront us. Yet, none of the nuclear weapons states has totally and categorically renounced the use of these weapons, and even the Chinese have hinted at some possibilities of first use.

Whether what has not happened from 1945 to 2005 can be counted upon to continue not happening hereafter is the central question of this book. The record of sixty years may be a great relief to all of us, but it does not serve as any perfect assurance. In this book we are not speculating so very much about a World War III, because that was brooded about a great deal during the Cold War. We must give some thought to more limited nuclear exchanges among the established nuclear powers but the same patterns and experience of deterrence that have so far prevented World War III will work to make "limited strategic nuclear war" somewhat less likely as well.

CHAPTER THREE

Likely World Reactions

Having outlined a variety of categories of nuclear escalation scenarios, we turn to speculating about how the world would react to these cases. If only because the scenarios are typically so horrible that no one wants to think about them, such reactions are indeed very difficult to predict. One can hope that the world will be brave and resolute, and also perceptive and responsible, so that the task of governments in responding to a breaking of the "nuclear taboo" will be easier. But we must also be prepared for much less helpful responses among peoples around the world. Given the worldwide trend toward the establishment of democracy, there will be many political leaders to whom such public reactions will be very important, because they will be facing the need to win reelection.

Responses everywhere may depend heavily on whether the nuclear weapon use was by a very marginal possessor of such weapons (we already noted above how this might affect the *physical* nature of the weapons) or by a major nuclear power (known to have a large stockpile, so not likely to have run down or exhausted its stock in launching the attack). If the initiator of nuclear warfare was an established nuclear weapons state, the attack might have utilized the state's strategic nuclear forces, or instead have involved only its tactical or theater nuclear forces; if the attack came from a state not even known beforehand to have possessed any nuclear weapons, the reactions would be different again.

These categories of attacker have to be arrayed against the categories of victim. The state suffering a nuclear attack might itself be a nuclear weapons state, which would suggest a high likelihood of nuclear retaliation, in continuing rounds of nuclear warfare. Very different outside reactions, and paths of appropriate policy, might emerge if the victim did not possess any nuclear weapons of its own.

Ambiguity about Whether the Line Was Crossed (Category A)

The first category of scenarios in our break-out above comprised the cases where nuclear escalation was difficult to define or the facts were difficult to determine. Was the Israeli attack on Osirak a nuclear escalation?[1] Today we do not remember it that way. If the fourth skyjacked airliner on September 11 was headed for Three Mile Island nuclear power plant, was this an attempted nuclear escalation? Again, whatever our shock at the events of that day, we do not quite see this attempt as a nuclear escalation.

For a hypothetical "near-miss" from the past, if the British Navy really had nuclear depth charges on board the ships engaged in combat around the Falklands, might Prime Minister Thatcher have been tempted to let her military commanders use such ASW munitions against the Argentine submarines that were threatening the success of the British expedition? Speculation about this counterfactual possibility (the possible response had the torpedoes fired by Argentine submarines against British ships exploded instead of failing to) was once answered by a knowledgeable specialist as follows: "How would the world have known if the British had used nuclear rather than conventional ASW?" since the evidence would not have been clear at the surface (although it might have come through clearly enough to all the acoustic listening stations monitoring the oceans of the world).[2]

Almost by definition, the world's reactions to ambiguity in these scenarios, for as long as it *remains* ambiguity, would be less reactions of shock; individuals and governments would perhaps be inclined to shrug off the news as rumor, so as to continue life as it was, to continue as if no violation of the taboo had occurred. Some such cases might be definitionally marginal but still very destructive to life, for example spreading radioactive nuclear waste materials across some wide area.

Cases with Surprisingly Low Collateral Damage (Category B)

The second group of escalation possibilities comprised cases in which nuclear weapons would be used in ways that caused little civilian harm. Contrary to what most of us normally expect, the first use of nuclear weapons since Nagasaki might (in a number of our scenarios) produce the reaction that "nothing so drastic" had happened, that nuclear weapons were in effect really "just another weapon," that no great changes in policy were required in response, as the appropriate attitude was a sort of "business as usual."

These are the scenarios, of course, where the nuclear weapon is *not* used to devastate a city, killing tens of thousands of people, but perhaps is used with no deaths at all (for example as a warhead for missile defense), or with no civilian deaths, as only a submarine and its crew are destroyed (a submarine that had been a target all along in conventional warfare).

As one measure of whether the publics and governments of the world, including the public of the United States, would go into a state of deep shock, we might adopt as our benchmark the reactions to the non-nuclear terrorist destruction of the World Trade Center on September 11, 2001. (It is a little early to tell whether Americans will regard the WTC attack as an event changing life as we knew it or as an event that can, with proper vigilance and a proper punitive response, be kept from happening again, that can be contained.[3]) Even though this benchmark is as yet a little difficult to sort out, we might nonetheless pose this test for a future nuclear event: Will the world's reactions to a particular nuclear escalation be less than were the American and other reactions to the WTC attack?

Terrorist attacks of the 9/11 type can have the impact of hardening everyone to other bad news. "Surprise" and "shock" are quite relative; they are based on a comparison with what one has come to expect. The nuclear escalation we are contemplating here, as we try to anticipate its consequences for the world, *could* thus come as a "pleasant surprise," if damage were relatively low-scale, and our worst fears through the years of the Cold War might then seem to have been excessive. We might wonder whether the nuclear taboo had not been based too much on excessive fears of the difference that nuclear weapons would make.

One thus has to pay at least some attention to the less shocking possibilities here, if only because the move to a minimally destructive nuclear escalation might indeed be the strategic approach of one of America's adversaries, such that it will be important for the United States to have devised its counteractions.

However, we should not be led into *counting upon* such a "not so bad news" outcome, since it is probable that nuclear escalation will turn out to be very bad news for all of us. Remaining much more likely would be the world reaction we have often anticipated, a reaction of shock and horror, of total pessimism and gloom, as a nuclear weapon is used in what seems like a repetition of Nagasaki or worse, with horrific totals of people killed and horrible images on live television of the wounded and dying. This reaction most definitely would see nuclear weapons *not* as ordinary weapons. This would be a confirmation of all the presumptions that nuclear weapons were qualitatively different.

Irresponsible Nuclear Escalations (Category C)

In our third set of cases, the ambiguity would not pertain to what happened (as in Category A) but to what the motivation was, to whether there was something accidental or inadvertent, or "crazy," about the nuclear event. This is a scenario for which we were somewhat more prepared (albeit hardly *well*-prepared) through all the years of the Cold War. Many people were concerned that a Soviet or American missile would be fired accidentally or that some commander would initiate nuclear war without receiving valid orders from his national command authority (these were the scenarios for such Hollywood movies as *Red Alert* and *Doctor Strangelove* and, more recently, *Crimson Tide*). The "hot line" connection between Washington and Moscow was presumably intended to serve somewhat as a remedy for this, but such scenarios still constitute a powerful argument for national missile defense systems.

The obvious point is that the world's reaction to this kind of a nuclear escalation (where the government whose warhead was detonated immediately claims that this was an accident or the act of crazy insubordination) would be confused: some people would be eager to accept the explanation, for fear that a failure to do so would bring further nuclear attack; others would want to impose retaliation in any event; but many people, depending on the past record of the country whose weapons were used, would be torn and not certain of what to do.

Because the enormous destructiveness normally associated with a nuclear attack makes a deliberate governmental decision to launch it so much less likely, such a crazy or insubordinate or terrorist launching of the nuclear attack may indeed be the most likely of the nuclear escalations we are anticipating in this study.

It might be wise for the established powers to pool their knowledge of the characteristics of existing nuclear weapons, the weapons that might be stolen and used by other states or by terrorist groups, creating a directory of the characteristics that would be displayed after an explosion and making it possible to identify at least the source of the bomb.[4] Coupled to this would be the programs already under way to reduce the risk of such weapons' being stolen. These programs rightly give aid particularly to the Russian authorities, who have to try to keep account of all the weapons that were assembled in the old Soviet Union.[5] They also assist countries like India and Pakistan with weapons inventorying techniques as well as command-and-control procedures.[6]

If a very destructive nuclear attack were to be launched entirely by physical accident, the world indeed might *not* be inclined thereafter to see nuclear warheads as "just another weapon" but rather as a very dangerous potential booby-trap, to be pushed further and further away from combat readiness.

Reactions to Mass Destruction: Preemptive Surrender? (Category D)

Our common sense is still that the most likely form of a nuclear attack will be the destruction of a city. The likely world responses to such a "very bad news" nuclear attack can come in a variety of forms.

The most worrisome possibility would be a desire by governments around the world to get off the target list, which would hardly be surprising when entire cities are at risk and could hardly be branded as cowardly. The desire to spare one's cities from nuclear attack has, after all, been at the core of mutual deterrence for all the years since 1949.

Countries might therefore adopt policies of retreat and preemptive surrender, leaving someone else to stand up to whoever had just used nuclear weapons. Pacifism, or a pseudo-pacifism that amounted merely to an aversion to suffering, might attract much support, especially in the democratic countries, where leaders had to win reelection, as well as in nondemocratic countries. If the United States were to take the lead in confronting the state that had initiated the attack, it might thus find itself losing some of its allies, as the publics of the world rationalized that the Americans were somehow at fault for the nuclear escalation or were at least morally to blame (because, if nothing else, Americans had invented nuclear weapons in the first place and had been the first and only prior power to use them). If the shock of the initial attack was great enough and it seemed that the nuclear escalator might be kept from further nuclear attacks if appeased enough and surrendered-to enough, the judgment of anyone opposing such appeasement might be denounced.

The seeming lack of enthusiasm for the Bush administration's 2003 push for a full disarmament of Saddam Hussein's weapons of mass destruction might suggest that the world would not be very resolute or very supportive of American or any other leadership if nuclear weapons were to be used somewhere around the world again.[7] It was clear that the Iraqi regime had reneged on the conditions by which it was offered a cease-fire in 1991, and still the world was not willing to force Saddam Hussein to adhere to his half of the bargain. Even the Iraqi ruler's grudging acceptance of a return of United Nations inspectors had come only because the United States was threatening to apply military force, and nevertheless tremendous opposition was expressed around the world, and even within the United States itself, to this brandishing of force.

Yet one could also draw a few more-optimistic suggestions from this real-life example. The evidence indeed indicated that Iraq had sought to acquire nuclear, biological, and chemical weapons. But the earlier experience from UN inspections suggested that disarmament had been plausibly complete and reliable at least on the nuclear dimension, the major remaining uncertainties and risks of Iraqi evasion pertaining instead to chemical and biological weapons.[8] This might show that the world still sees nuclear weapons as uniquely threatening, biological attack as yet having no Hiroshima and Nagasaki equivalent to make it more real. In short, the evidence of 2003 cannot predict the world's response to an *actual use* of nuclear weapons; it shows only an irresolute world response to an Iraqi move that was mostly toward the possession of non-nuclear weapons.

The reactions of the French, German, Russian, and Chinese governments, and of the British public, to the American pressure on Baghdad are thus not very encouraging, but also not definitively discouraging, when we try to project whether the world would follow American leadership in responding to a nuclear aggression.

It has to be conceded, of course, that some of the uneven backing that the Bush administration has drawn from NATO and other allies, and even from the American population itself, stems from the "unilateralist" tone that Bush adopted during the 2000 election campaign and then persisted with thereafter, a tone with a great deal of reference to the "American interests," which would be pursued ahead of other nations' interests, as the administration, even before the attacks of September 11th, proclaimed the United States willing to act without the approval of other nations and free to reject the advice of others.[9]

Pursuing one's own interests is an abstraction that can become a tautology, because every country in some broad sense does this; even when cooperating with allies and following their advice, a country will do what serves its own interests. But for the U.S. administration to make such a large point of how it would act independently, reducing its consultation with the world community and other states, was more than a tautology, for it suggested that Bush and his advisers found many of the policies of predecessor administrations to be a bad service of American interests. If the new tone of the United States government sent a signal that Bush found American interests increasingly at odds with those of Japan and Western Europe and the other democracies, it would be natural to expect such countries to be more reluctant to follow American leadership.[10]

The Iraqi invasion of Kuwait in 1990 was a major shock to the international system, and it was followed by the world's rallying behind the United States in response. Saddam Hussein's failure to cooperate with UN inspectors by contrast came as less of a shock.[11]

But, to address the major point of this analysis, a use of nuclear weapons anywhere around the world, under most circumstances, would produce an even more major shock than the Iraqi aggression of 1991.

Less Defeatist Responses to a Rogue State Attack (Category E)

Rather than any rush to surrender, very much the opposite reaction to the shock of a nuclear attack on a city might emerge, that such an escalation required enormous punishment of the perpetrator and an enormous effort to change the world so that such an attack would not be repeated.

This reaction would signify a perception, among publics and in governments, that assertiveness and retaliation were most urgently needed, that patience and appeasement could not be appropriate once the nuclear-use line had been crossed, and that the judgment of the military professionals might have to take precedence over that of diplomats and other civilians. Here we would expect to hear demands for unconditional surrender, regime change, or total disarmament of the nuclear culprit, as most of the world would want to terminate the nuclear exchange as quickly as possible and at the same time (not always a compatible goal) to establish that such behavior will not be tolerated in the future.[12]

Two-Sided Nuclear Wars (Category F)

One of the more horrible prospects for the world would come in an introduction of nuclear weapons on both sides of a hostile confrontation, as between today's India and Pakistan, an exchange in which each side was trying to preempt the other's next round of attacks and at the same time retaliate for the last round. Millions of people might perish every single day.

While the case can be made that such an exchange might convey less horror in parts of the world far from the target and with a very different culture, the processes of global news coverage and global interaction today virtually guarantee that the world would be aghast at such an exchange, no matter where it occurred. One can almost count on news operations such as CNN to expend great efforts to bring the horror home to all the living rooms of the world.[13]

The worldwide reaction in this case would indeed be to pray for an early ending of the exchange, for the point where one side's nuclear arsenal had been exhausted and/or preemptively destroyed, and to welcome any steps that could shorten such a war.

The Use of Established Nuclear Arsenals (Category G)

As noted several times, a most important factor would be whether the nuclear escalation was launched by a major nuclear power, a power which would retain a large nuclear force even after it had fired one or several rounds. (For historical reasons, we normally think of Russia here, more than of Britain or France, or even of China at its current level of nuclear armament, but this may change as Beijing expands its nuclear arsenal.)

The outside world would want to punish the nuclear attack but at the same time steer the incentives of the aggressor, so as to avoid provoking additional nuclear attacks. The management of this has always been complicated,[14] and the strategic calculation of such management, analyzed all through the Cold War, has always been difficult, because one has to find just the right retaliatory targets and still leave other targets untouched—as hostages kept alive to assure restraint by the guilty party. This involves a deep analysis of the priorities the adversary assigns to various of its assets.

The task has also been difficult in terms of human psychology, as Americans have not adjusted easily to the logic of "limited war," by which one fights with some weapons and not with others, by which one hits only certain targets on the other side.[15] When feelings of anger and revenge well up, one does not like to be told that one has to negotiate with, and engage in tacit bargaining with, the government that has just destroyed one of your cities in a nuclear attack.

Blurrings and Blendings of Categories

There may well be instances of nuclear escalation which straddle the boundaries sorted out in the above categories, thereby producing additional confusion as to which responses would be appropriate. What if a use of nuclear weapons were at the same time low in damage to civilians, and uncertain as to whether it was truly "nuclear," and unclear as to who had launched it? What if an aggression utilizing nuclear weapons was launched by a democracy? What if nuclear weapons were used brutally against a city but the user was clearly the defender, the victim of aggression? These would be cases where our normal instincts and expectations would be conflicted, working against each other. We must always be prepared for variations that might otherwise have gone totally unanticipated.

The Impact on World Acceptance
of American Leadership

The various reactions to a nuclear escalation may now be translated into impacts on the world's attitudes about the leadership role of the United States. A multinational instinct toward retreat would mean less world support for Washington as an alliance leader, and it might even mean a total termination of some alliances or just an erosion of their effectiveness.[16]

If most countries seemed to be attaching their highest priority to protecting themselves against nuclear attack, a few would therefore urgently seek to acquire nuclear weapons of their own, or, if this were too difficult a task, would perhaps reach for chemical or biological weapons as a "poor man's H-bomb," a weapon of mass destruction to hit back with or use as a deterrent threat.

The erosion of alliances and the isolation of the formerly protected might thus breed a general pattern of individual self-defense rather than any reliance on collective security arrangements, or reliance on mutual security alliances. If the American public were itself seen to be giving in to an "every man for himself" reaction to nuclear escalation, or even if this reaction were mostly showing up elsewhere, any inclination to follow American leadership would be reduced.

Conversely, if the instinctive response to nuclear escalation were less toward surrender and appeasement and more toward corrective reaction, this could be a strong reinforcement for existing alliances and for American leadership (on the proviso, of course, that the United States was not itself succumbing to defeatism and fear in face of a nuclear attack).

An interesting model for how the latter would work has been the events after September 11, 2001. The initial responses from China and Russia, as well as those from France and India, surprised many by the degree of support given to President Bush and the United States campaign against the Taliban and Al Qaeda. The attack on the World Trade Center, at least initially, served as a sort of "validating shock" for existing alliances and for the expansion of alliances, to the point that President Putin of Russia even voiced a lowering of opposition to NATO expansion and many saw the possibility also of a decisive shift of Sino-American relations into a more positive path.[17]

The "validating shock" of a *nuclear* detonation (unless the detonation was so carefully conducted that much less damage was done than at the WTC) would most likely be in the same direction, and of greater magnitude. The gravity of such diplomatic revolutions is always difficult to gauge at the time they are occurring, and it is too early to assess the real impact of the terrorist attacks on decision making in Moscow or Beijing. But, just as in the September 11th case, the world might, after a nuclear attack, experience a surprising reshuffling and expansion of alliances.

Great importance will thus attach to whether NATO and the other alliances of which the United States is a party will stick together. And similar importance will attach to whether the permanent members of the United Nations Security Council will stick together, as they did for Desert Storm and in the immediate aftermath of the September 11th attack, because the legitimation provided by Security Council resolutions has not been trivial in guiding how the democracies of the world see things.

The risks of nuclear weapons proliferation, and of nuclear weapons *use*, hovered over two crises the United States faced in 2003, the crises with North Korea and with Iraq. In each case a dictatorial regime that had previously behaved outrageously with regard to the outside world was again defying the world, by reneging on the promises and international control arrangements by which it had renounced nuclear weapons.

Some critics of American policy choices indeed fault the priorities set in Washington by which Iraq was deemed as requiring more immediate action than North Korea. A portion of such criticism, within the United States and outside, may have reflected only an opposition's fault-finding attack on the Bush administration, such that either arrangement of priorities would have been criticized and the Republicans accused of looking for trouble abroad. But other critics noted that nuclear weapons proliferation could be excluded in the Iraqi case for the moment, while it could not at all in the North Korean case, and that nuclear threats still posed much more of a risk of disaster.

The eruption of crises with two such adversaries at the same time (to be repeated in 2005 as the United States confronted North Korea and Iran) was hardly unpredictable, even if the two American adversaries did not communicate with each other extensively and there were no conspiracy between them. The elementary principles of the balance of power have always suggested that any more minor state might feel freer to defy the will of a hegemon when another minor state was also acting defiantly. Critics of defense spending have long scoffed at the Pentagon's demanding the ability to fight "two and a half wars," wondering where this index came from; it stemmed straightforwardly from the same logic that a century earlier had persuaded Britain to maintain a fleet as large as the next two fleets combined.[18]

Critics of hegemonic power—of British might in the nineteenth century or American power in the twenty-first—will argue that such power produces arrogance, as the interests of the hegemon are served to the neglect of the interests of other states. But the track record of the United States (and indeed of Britain earlier) does not support so completely the advocacy of international balance-of-power policies. The past record of American behavior might instead support bandwagoning, by which the world realizes that global interests have been served, not just those of the hegemon.[19]

There will always be French, Russian, Chinese, and Indian analysts of international relations who adopt a "realist" line of reasoning by which American power requires counterbalancing, by which American initiatives are seen to serve American purposes to the detriment of the needs of the rest of the world.[20] It is unfortunate when American analysts adopt a similar "realist" rhetoric that reinforces such suspicions abroad.

Yet it is not easy to find people in these countries who would really welcome, or even be indifferent to, a North Korean, Iraqi, or Iranian acquisition of nuclear weapons, for they are quite aware that these are regimes which may be prone to use such weapons, once they are acquired.

Leaving aside the tactical issues of whether the Bush administration has properly advertised its role in the world, as the proliferation and use of nuclear weapons must be contained, the difficulties of 2003 illustrate as well the inherent limits of American conventional military power. Even with the best management of interalliance relations, it might have been difficult to muster meaningful military threats against *both* Baghdad and Pyongyang, and then also Tehran. In the euphoria at the end of the Cold War, it was assumed that the American military forces could be drastically downsized, that they would in fact be seeking new roles in "military operations other than war" (MOOTW). This expectation is very much contradicted by the possibilities being addressed here—that nuclear weapons may proliferate despite the best efforts of the existing non-proliferation arrangements and that such proliferation would add unhappily to the prospects and scenarios in which such weapons would be *used*.[21]

Responses around the System

Also important will be the responses of the other possessors of nuclear weapons, as they consider whether to imitate any nuclear escalation that has occurred, as they judge whether there is some lesson to be learned here, a lesson on how to exploit the world to one's own advantage by actually employing a nuclear weapon.

One may see cases in which the perpetrator of the nuclear attack is "sorry" for the attack, in one way or another, perhaps because it was truly accidental or an act of insubordination, perhaps because the immediate world reaction is so hostile that the government that launched the attack realizes it has made a colossal mistake and must make amends as quickly as possible. If the next use of nuclear weapons were to be followed by a general perception that this had been a grievous mistake, even in terms of the self-interest of the state which had initiated the escalation, the world would then perhaps see a reinforcement for the nuclear taboo rather than an erosion.

The potential "copy cats" will thus be closely watching any instance of nuclear weapons use, just as they watched Saddam Hussein's conventional aggression of 1990, just as they were watching Osama bin Laden's terrorist attack on New York in 2001, to see whether such acts pay off, whether this is something one can get away with.

How the major powers react, how the minor powers react, how states similarly inclined toward the status quo and law and order react, will affect how much a new use of nuclear weapons will be a major model for future behavior and how much it can be contained.

A Total Change in World Outlook?

The most likely version of nuclear escalation, when all is said and done, may remain the attack in which many people are killed and many wounded, when the world again feels the horror of Hiroshima and Nagasaki but this time without the tempering effect of its following years of world war.

It is thus certainly possible, among all the uncertainties we have to consider, that the first new use of nuclear weapons would produce such widespread horror that all the possessors of nuclear weapons would be *less* likely again to use them (perhaps including the perpetrator of the event, perhaps even if the perpetrator is neither punished nor disarmed). Rather than destroying the taboo and setting a new precedent, this could, by a demonstration of the dreadful consequences, therefore be a reinforcement of the taboo. Such a next use of nuclear weapons would refresh our memories of Hiroshima and Nagasaki.

If the perpetrator of the attack itself recoils in a seemingly genuine horror, striving desperately to redefine its initiative as an accident or as an insubordination or act of preemptive panic (perhaps renouncing any territorial gains it might have obtained in the process and offering to contribute to the relief of the damages), the world may feel less need to punish the action. A certain self-policing "common sense" might then settle in by which this kind of military initiative would not be taken again.

One must remember how remarkable the world's abstinence from nuclear escalation since 1945 has been and how much this has been the product of our genuine dismay at the suffering of the two Japanese cities. The horror was more than a little mitigated by worldwide relief at the quick ending of a long and massively destructive conventional war, but it still has been the base for the generally accepted qualitative distinction between nuclear and conventional weapons. The human victims at Hiroshima and Nagasaki may have been crucial to post-1949 mutual deterrence as we have known it.[22]

Advocates of peace and of disarmament are often too optimistic in assuming that the mere contemplation of the horror of war will lead nations to remain at peace. But even the "tough-minded realist" cannot dismiss the political impact of the dread of war, and especially the next instance of *nuclear* war. The next use of nuclear weapons could conceivably reinforce peace thereafter, rather than undermining it.

Total Nuclear Disarmament?

There are some analysts who would even predict that any further use of nuclear weapons would finally bestir the world to make the appropriate moves and take the necessary risks to achieve a nuclear-weapons-free world.[23] These observers allege that the fact that something like Nagasaki could happen again would convince one and all that these weapons are so abominable that the world will not tolerate their use or even their existence. China, Russia, and the United States would join Britain and France in committing to a verifiable move to zero nuclear weapons and would together coerce Israel, Pakistan, and India, and whoever else to match this.

But such expectations are almost surely unrealistic.[24] The shock and horror of a use of nuclear weapons, especially if it were directed at a city, would indeed be great—great enough to shake us all out of traditional paths of thinking. But the traditional objections to nuclear disarmament would still have to be overcome, most specifically the problems of verification and the risks that someone would cheat to retain a rudimentary nuclear arsenal and then be free to dictate the political future of the world, if everyone else had gone ahead with nuclear disarmament. The mere possibility of such cheating, probably amid rumors of the imperfections in the control system, might cause other states to contemplate cheating themselves; and a chain of self-confirming hypotheses would then emerge, as everyone had to fear the worst case of behavior by the other states, and in the process confirmed the fears of others.

There might indeed be no better way to *increase* the likelihood of nuclear weapons' coming into use than to take such a plunge toward total nuclear disarmament.[25] The mutual fears of cheating would soon enough lead to mutual fears of preemptive nuclear attack, all of these being the kinds of fears that were easy to dismiss when the nuclear arsenals of Russia and the United States remained so very large but could not be dismissed now.

Also, a nuclear escalation might cause Washington and Moscow to renew building their own nuclear arsenals, since such weapons would again be of great political and military relevance. Depending only a little on what kind of nuclear weapon was used in what kind of attack, the existing nuclear weapons states might well feel prodded to increase still more their inventory of smaller nuclear warheads, warheads capable of fulfilling military requirements without imposing as much collateral damage on civilian targets.[26]

The Impact on Weapons Proliferation

An extremely important category of the anticipated aftermath of a nuclear escalation would be the impact on further nuclear proliferation, the spread of nuclear weapons possession to additional countries, and, conversely, the impact on the nonproliferation effort tailored to preventing or reducing such spread. If the *use* of nuclear weapons leads to a wider *possession* of such weapons, this would in turn increase the chances of further use, in a spiral that could be disastrous.

Looking at the pessimistic possibilities, it is very plausible that several countries that had previously elected *not* to acquire nuclear weapons would reverse their decision after an actual breaking of the nuclear taboo. Japan would probably be near the top of the list for a variety of reasons, but there are European and Latin American states as well that once considered acquiring such weapons and then moved away from them, in face of international opinion, and domestic opinion, that such weapons were no longer a natural accessory to sovereignty, that such weapons were not "just another weapon."[27] Especially if the user of nuclear weapons got away with something that would not have been possible without such nuclear escalation, and especially if the United States and the other established nuclear weapons states did not support the country that had lacked such weapons, the message would seem to be that even the most peace-minded of countries had better apply itself to acquiring a nuclear arsenal, in a world where such weapons had been used again.

A very different result would emerge, of course, if the user of nuclear weapons did *not* win battles and conquer territory in the process and did not induce the United States and other powers to back away from their commitments to a system of collective security. If the user were simply to produce its own defeat and to be subjected then to total conquest and regime change, the political factions from country to country opposing a policy of nuclear proliferation would be reinforced. The simple shock and horror of the nuclear destruction of a city could indeed galvanize the world into doing more than trying to punish the immediate perpetrator, inducing a much more aggressive nonproliferation effort, perhaps even a de-proliferation effort.[28] One must remember how enormous the shock of the next use of nuclear weapons might be, perhaps shaking public opinion in all the major countries out of their established tracks.

The model might be the efforts at the beginning of the twenty-first century directed at precluding nuclear and other weapons of mass destruction in Iraq and North Korea and Iran, but hypothetically with a much less half-hearted backing from the powers outside the United States. The agenda might include far more intrusive inspections by the International Atomic Energy Agency and far stricter controls over sales and exports of nuclear material. And the agenda might even include the elimination of some *existing* nuclear arsenals, for example, those of Pakistan or Israel.

A total nuclear disarmament remains unlikely. A rush toward nuclear proliferation, as every country retreats into looking out for itself, is among the more pessimistic forecasts. But a more resolute effort at limiting the number of states having nuclear weapons, given the near-global consensus that had emerged in the 1980s and 1990s about the dangers of nuclear proliferation, is among the more hopeful possibilities.

The event we are focusing on, the first use of a nuclear weapon since Nagasaki, could thus basically have two opposite effects on the *horizontal* proliferation of nuclear weapons. One response could easily be that even Japan and Germany would elect to acquire such weapons and that there would be a helter-skelter outward proliferation, as the number of states possessing such weapons moved well into double digits. Especially if the victim of the nuclear attack was a state without nuclear weapons, hence unable to retaliate in kind, the lesson for the world might be that one needs a nuclear arsenal to fend off this kind of attack. (Where the victim of the nuclear attack had been one of the nuclear weapons states, however, a somewhat opposite lesson could be extracted, that possessing such weapons does not guarantee deterrence, does not necessarily protect one's cities and armed forces against becoming nuclear victims.)

A very different response to nuclear escalation would be if the major powers then agreed to a massive new effort to halt proliferation, including military action to preempt it if ordinary diplomacy could not be persuasive.

Compared to the "shock response" of total nuclear disarmament (which may indeed have to be consigned to a never-never world, because of all the problems of verification), this kind of drastic-action world response may be *more* plausible. The shock and horror of a nuclear attack might seem to disprove the argument presented so often by Indians and Pakistanis, and by some other advocates of nuclear proliferation, that mutual deterrence can work all around the world now just as well as it worked during the Cold War between the United States and the Soviet Union.[29] The major powers, very possibly backed by the authority of the United Nations Security Council, might launch outright military attacks to keep additional countries from getting nuclear weapons (perhaps even using their own nuclear weapons in such attacks).

One might similarly see preemptive interventions against any state already possessing nuclear weapons which seemed politically about to fall to pieces (a prime current example perhaps being Pakistan), since the fear of what might be done with such weapons in the chaos of rioting and civil war would have been so much reinforced by a real-life example of nuclear weapons use.

Moving away from the ups and downs of *nuclear* proliferation, the world's response to a nuclear weapons use might be a frenzied race to acquire chemical and biological weapons, as states seek an alternative retaliatory instrument to deter any nuclear attack on themselves. Much would depend on whether the original victim of nuclear attack had brought it on by a use of CBW, for the lesson might instead be that the brandishing of any kind of weapon of mass destruction simply makes one a nuclear target, all the WMD being lumped together as a category. But, if the original victim of the nuclear attack had lacked *all* WMD, chemical and biological as well as nuclear, the lesson emerging would rather be that the world has become dangerous for anyone lacking *some* means of deterrence.

If the nuclear escalation we are considering involved the employment of a missile delivery system, this almost certainly would enhance the appeal of antimissile systems around the world, in any country that could afford such a system. This would be especially true if the nuclear escalation had been *thwarted* by a theater missile defense system, the incoming nuclear warhead being destroyed or diverted from its intended city target by the firing of a defensive missile. And it might be just as true if the victim of the attack had been a country which had elected to remain defenseless against a missile strike, not investing in any antimissile defenses.

A somewhat opposite tendency would appear if the nuclear attack had gotten around an *ineffective* missile defense, thus conveying the lesson that nuclear warheads make such defenses pointless even if the impact of the incoming missile were diverted by a half-mile, for cities would be destroyed and many thousands of people killed in any event. It is very uncertain whether missile defenses will be effective, and *remain* effective, over the coming decades.

Turning finally to the world's feelings about *conventional* armaments and conventional warfare, some might conclude that nuclear escalation would shift the priorities away from conventional warfare preparations, as nuclear weapons would have been reactivated as the trump suit. Yet the counterconclusion might be that the horror suffered in the nuclear attack would greatly reduce the aversion that Americans and Europeans have displayed in recent decades to the loss of soldiers in armed combat. We have seen this already in the American response to the attack on the World Trade Center. When thousands of civilians had just been killed in a U.S. city, Americans did not shrink from suffering casualties in Afghanistan, whereas in Somalia, the loss of even some dozens of American soldiers in ground combat was enough to make the American public favor a retreat.[30] The aversion to combat deaths would not apply if nuclear weapons had been used against an American target, and it might not apply even if someone else in the world had been hit with a nuclear attack.

Countries around the world may thus feel the need to be more ready for *all* kinds of war, including conventional war, after a nuclear weapon had been used. Except if a state were to choose retreat and preemptive surrender (wanting to get its forces out of any forward bases abroad for fear that such bases could become nuclear targets, etc.), the powers would need to retain and augment their conventional forces.

There may be a need to respond to a nuclear attacker with *conventional* means, and the apparent cost of conventional warfare efforts, including conventional casualties, will have gone down because of the introduction of nuclear destruction in the background.

Japan in Particular

If another use of nuclear weapons is avoided, the United States would remain the unique user of nuclear weapons. And, obviously, Japan would remain the unique victim of nuclear attack. It follows that one important consequence of the scenarios we have been discussing here is that with any further nuclear attack Japan's role would be changed, and very possibly, as a result, Japan's attitudes on nuclear proliferation. Unless Japan were *again* to be the nuclear victim, it would no longer have this special status to work with in its dialogues with the world.

Japanese nongovernmental organizations, and indeed also the spokesmen for the Japanese government itself, have been quite adept since 1945 in harnessing the sympathy of the outside world for what happened at Hiroshima and Nagasaki, with the net impact of this, either as a natural flow of logic or as a more manipulated flow, being to erase most American anger about Pearl Harbor and about the treatment of American prisoners of war in World War II. Japan's declarations of non-nuclear status, its professions of being afflicted with a special "nuclear allergy," its adherence to the nuclear Non-Proliferation Treaty, and its insistence that the United States never declare that it has nuclear weapons on board any vessel or aircraft using Japanese bases have been very consistent with reminding the world that it *alone* has suffered nuclear devastation.[31] The outside world has been grateful for Japan's "nuclear allergy," as a source of Japanese restraint; but the world, in particular the United States, has also been much less resentful than one would expect of Japan's role in World War II, and less critical of its unwillingness to accept very much guilt for this history, in its schoolbooks or its general political discourse.

But, if nuclear weapons are used in South Asia or in the Middle East, or anywhere else except again against Japan, the power of this special historical experience will be significantly muted in Japan's dialogue with other nations, and the balance of considerations by which Japan has elected to forswear nuclear weapons will be altered. The use of nuclear weapons anywhere will threaten the barriers to nuclear *proliferation* all around the world, but the logic noted here would move Japan to relatively high on the list of states for which there would be a new proliferation concern.

This would be particularly true, of course, if nuclear weapons were to be used anywhere geographically near Japan, on the Korean Peninsula or in some sort of a conflict around Taiwan, for instance. But there would be a problem for Japan even if the nuclear escalation occurred on the other side of the globe. If a city were to be hit anywhere in the world, the special status of the annual commemorations at Hiroshima and Nagasaki would be reduced; and Japan's involvement with the "nuclear card" would have to shift from attracting sympathy and inculcating American and Western guilt to an exploiting of Japan's potential for producing nuclear weapons of its own.

Even at the end of the twentieth century, the Japanese government had been drawing criticism for pursuing the reprocessing of plutonium, some of its spokesmen purporting to be unaware that such plutonium could be used for nuclear weapons as well as for reactor fuel.[32] The plutonium involved was much more expensive than the alternative of acquiring partially enriched uranium from foreign sources, so Japanese explanations that such policies were a simple hedge against possible future price rises in alternative fuels drew skepticism. The ratios of costs to insurance back-ups were not at all consistent with other business practices. Japan in the same decade was also investing in the rocket technology for placing satellites into orbit, even though the established American, Russian, or French capacities in this field could have orbited such satellites at a much lower cost. A wary observer of these Japanese decisions would conclude that, taken together, these were investments in a latent short-lead-time nuclear missile capability, as Japan would now always be just months, not years, away from the ability to inflict nuclear retaliation on Pyongyang or Beijing.[33]

One hardly needs to belabor the proliferation consequences if the next city destroyed anywhere around the world in a nuclear attack were to be a *Japanese* city. Rather than simply adding one more Japanese place name to the intonation of Hiroshima and Nagasaki and renewing the Japanese "nuclear allergy," the result would more probably be a Japanese decision to acquire nuclear weapons, to be sure that there would be no such attacks in the future.

Yet it is by no means certain that any breaking of the nuclear taboo around the globe would increase the chances of Japan's acquiring nuclear weapons. Much would depend, as always, on how the United States responded to such an event, on whether the United States' posture of extended nuclear deterrence on behalf of Japan seemed to be continuing. An American "nuclear umbrella" has been seen as protecting Japan against a conventional invasion, in case the Soviets or anyone else acquired the amphibious capability for invading Japan, and as protecting Japan against nuclear attack, with the willingness of the United States to use nuclear weapons in defense of its valued ally precluding any need for Japan to develop nuclear forces of its own.[34]

If the United States were to respond resolutely to a nuclear attack on a target somewhere else around the world, the Japanese interest might seem to lie in continuing to voice the "nuclear allergy" that has been a staple of Japanese political discourse ever since 1945, including a reminder to the world that Japan has been history's only nuclear victim, a renunciation of Japanese accquisition of such weapons, and a general desire to be unaware of and not involved in the deployments of American nuclear weapons. If the American people and government were to shrink from confronting the state that had used such weapons, however, Japanese thinking could shift in very much the opposite direction.

Much would depend also on the reaction of the rest of the world. If world opinion condemned the nuclear escalation that took place and if the use of such weapons seemed basically ineffective, the influence of those favoring Japanese nuclear weapons would not be strengthened. If the opposite held true, Japan might indeed surge toward the front of the list of new proliferators.

CHAPTER FOUR

Likely American
Popular Reactions

The probable responses of the American public to a use of nuclear weapons fall into the same seven categories of scenarios. There are possibilities of ambiguity at various levels of analysis. While an escalation might come in a form that was a "pleasant surprise," most of us would expect a great horror and shock, generating a variety of responses.

Ambiguity about Whether the Line
Was Crossed (Category A)

All that was said earlier about global confusion as to whether we had a real case of nuclear escalation (based on difficulties of definition, or difficulties of establishing the evidence) will apply for Americans. The United States government is surely equipped with the best intelligence-gathering devices to help determine the truth or falsity of an allegation that nuclear weapons had been used (e.g., if Britain had used a nuclear depth-charge to destroy an Argentine submarine, it might have been mostly American sensor operators whose hearing was damaged by the underwater signal of the detonation). Yet, given the vastness of the globe and the possible ingenuity of nuclear weapons designers producing future "mini-nukes," there may still be cases that are hard to resolve. And, for good reasons, the United States government cannot share all the information it has with foreign governments, or with the American public.

The United States similarly leads the world in the extent to which its strategic analysts, inside and outside the government, have thought through the logic of the distinction between conventional and nuclear warfare. Yet the possible definitional ambiguities noted at the outset remain.

Perhaps the U.S. government will know more than the American public about what has happened, but the possibility that ordinary Americans would feel unsure about whether a nuclear escalation had occurred is hardly unimportant for U.S. foreign policy. An important part of the nuclear taboo, of the general global abstention from the use of such weapons, is based on what the world's publics, including the American public, *think* about the question, since perceptions can be so self-confirming and self-renewing.

In a case of popular ambiguity, the public might try to round the uncertainties down to zero by concluding that "nothing really happened." The policy questions would then pertain to whether this was bad or good for American national interests and how long this impression could be maintained.

We mentioned earlier the uncertainty, often rounded down to zero, about whether there was a nuclear test over the South Atlantic in 1979, conducted by Israel or South Africa. A much broader ambiguity about the violation of a taboo has pertained for all these years about whether Israel, with or without an actual test detonation, actually possesses nuclear weapons. The United States and Israel, and the rest of the world, seem to have settled into an acceptance of ambiguity on that question, preferring ambiguity to some kind of clarification.[1] Might the same choice be the appropriate policy response to some future ambiguity about whether one state or another had *used* a nuclear weapon?

Cases with Surprisingly Low Collateral Damage (Category B)

In another scenario, Americans will *not* be terribly shocked by the next use of nuclear weapons, will not remember exactly where they were standing when they heard the news. Much of this would depend on the physical proximity of the nuclear attack. If it were far removed from North America, with no CNN television cameras around, and/or if the nuclear attack were purely or mostly on military targets (for example, an earth-penetrator warhead to destroy a military or terrorist underground command post), the American reaction might indeed be that "nuclear weapons were just another weapon." If the target were closer and the damage more visible, with a city being hit and tens of thousands killed and wounded, the reaction would instead be very great shock. The pictures of Hiroshima and Nagasaki were graphic enough to condition decades of Americans and others to regard nuclear war as uniquely horrible; a new round of such pictures of dead and wounded would almost surely reinforce this impression.

The American public would of course be considerably less offended if the initiator of nuclear warfare was an ally or friend of the United States and if the occasion for such nuclear escalation had been some outrage by the opposing side (e.g., a massive use of chemical or biological weapons or a conventional attack intended to wipe out the American ally). If the nuclear response seemed commensurate, and especially if the nuclear attack was kept low on the scale of collateral damage to civilians, there would be much more chance of American popular approval of the action, and of an equanimity with the fact that nuclear weapons had again been put to use.

Always to be included in the array of possibilities is that it might even have been *American* nuclear weapons that had been used.[2] While many Americans would still be shocked by such a breaking of the nuclear taboo (and while a few Americans react almost instinctively against *any* American military initiative), the majority of Americans would be much more likely to assume that there had been a good reason to treat nuclear weapons as "another weapon" rather than as something never to be used.

Irresponsible Nuclear Escalations (Category C)

If the nuclear attack is described as an accident by the government whose warhead was used, or as an insubordinate act by an officer who had gone berserk, American opinion could be counted upon to be confused and divided. Some would suspect that this was an excuse (as with earlier more minor cases of state-sponsored terrorism, so that the national leader was shielded by a "plausible deniability") and would demand retaliation in any event, or at least major reforms of the decision process in the state involved, as well as major compensation. Others might be quick to accept the explanation, especially if the nuclear attack did not seem to make particular sense in terms of the national interest of the country whose bomb was involved.

Having been conditioned to the subject by years of concern over the command-and-control of *American* nuclear weapons and by the analogous logics of the role of insanity versus personal responsibility in domestic criminal law, many Americans might want to be somewhat patient about the launching of retaliation.[3]

It even remains possible that a nuclear explosion could occur somewhere in the world without its being known who had set it off or whose nuclear weapon had been used.[4]

Reactions to Mass Destruction: Preemptive Surrender? (Category D)

The use of nuclear weapons against a city would most probably hit Americans as a major shock, as an event very inconsistent with what had been happening in the world just before such an attack, and this makes the American reaction, whether toward retreat or toward reaction and greater intervention, inherently difficult to predict.

Within the United States, one might see some very defeatist and retreatist sentiments, especially if the United States had not yet been a target of nuclear attack, with *some* Americans arguing that the highest priority should be protecting American cities, even if this meant avoiding intervention in conflicts abroad, even if this meant that we could not protect or rescue the victims of aggression or protect our traditional allies. Calls might emerge for withdrawals from American military bases abroad, the bases where so many young American military personnel would be packed together as easy targets, the bases that might irritate and anger someone who had just demonstrated a willingness to employ nuclear weapons.

In any event, the American public might be more than a little divided here, just as it was in the days before the Pearl Harbor attack and in the weeks before American entry into World War I.[5] Adversaries of the United States have historically been misled about American intentions in case after case and have underrated the American willingness to defend allies or to persevere in the endurance contest of an ongoing war.[6] The Japanese decision to launch World War II underestimated the American willingness to carry such a war through to a conclusion. The North Korean invasion of South Korea in 1950 misread American willingness to defend the ROK; the Soviet 1978 invasion of Afghanistan and Saddam Hussein's 1990 invasion of Kuwait were similarly based on a misreading of likely American responses.

If nuclear weapons are introduced into combat somewhere by a power hostile to the United States, or even by a power whose relations with the United States are more neutral, it is thus very likely that such a power will have underestimated the American response to such an escalation.

As is always the case in political democracies, much would depend on whether the nuclear escalation happened close to an election. Opposing candidates would try to contribute to the national interest as they took stands on domestic and foreign policy, while at the same time having to be very intent on winning voters to their side.[7] If the nuclear escalation came just after a president had been elected with a clear and substantial mandate, it might be easier for that president to be straightforwardly forceful in response to the event. If the attack occurred instead while two candidates were locked in a close and bitter campaign, each might have to take the more cautious and frightened portion of the American public into account.

The American response would also depend on the caliber of the people holding office in the democracies of the world. Some presidents and prime ministers have extensive experience with and interest in world affairs, while others come into office regarding foreign policy as a distraction to be avoided as much as possible. Some leaders will be adept at handling the tensions of an international crisis, while others will not. It is hard to imagine a crisis that would be as taxing as a new use of nuclear weapons.

There are many around the world who would see nuclear escalation as something to blame on the United States, for no other reason than that this country was the first to develop and use nuclear weapons, and there are also Americans who would accept this kind of analysis. Some of such Americans would react, as they have in other international confrontations, against the U.S. military and anything that smacks of "strategy." If the nuclear escalation seemed to auger threats of additional nuclear attacks, and on the United States itself or overseas American bases, many Americans might lean toward a policy of withdrawal, of avoiding the wrath of those proven ready to use nuclear weapons. A larger slice of the American population is more likely to reject this kind of defeatist reasoning, especially if there had already been a nuclear attack on the United States itself or on a close American ally and if the attacker was thought to have been a more minor power or a terrorist.

Some Americans would see ties to Israel or Taiwan or any other ally as a source of nuclear risk and would favor abandonment of these allies as the way to avoid nuclear destruction. This would be a pattern of preemptive surrender and retreat from commitments, perhaps the fondest dream of the adversary regime that had used nuclear weapons. But other Americans would react to a nuclear escalation by a conclusion that "we are all in this together," that "there is no escape," because the perpetrators hate what the United States stands for, regardless of its immediate policies, and because nuclear weapons by their very nature can be delivered to targets within the United States from anywhere on earth, so that isolating oneself from potential battlefields is not an option.

The bleakest picture of American responses to someone's use of nuclear weapons is that of an American withdrawal or retreat from the world, an even more obvious and craven retreat than the American reversion to isolationism in the 1920s. The American isolationism after World War I was not based on any blow or defeat Americans had suffered (although there was a widespread unhappiness about the high casualties among American forces after they entered combat against the Germans along the trench lines in France) but on a disillusionment with the motives and practices of the American partners in the war.[8] A withdrawal after an American target had suffered a nuclear attack, or a withdrawal merely in fear of such an attack, would strike many around the world more as a sign of American cowardice and surrender than as a mere disillusionment with the motives of other countries.

More likely than a simple withdrawal would be an American emphasis on unilateralism, on the United States' making its own decisions without extensively consulting other countries, an extended version of the tone attributed to the Bush administration when it came into office in January of 2001.[9]

At the most immediate level, the American public might sense that American bases, like those on Diego Garcia and Guam, and American aircraft carriers would make tempting targets for nuclear attack once the precedent had been set that nuclear weapons were again usable. This is a judgment that might also be made by many military professionals.

The sentiment might be strong for the deployment of theater missile defenses (TMD) to shield such forward troop deployments, but there would also be some widespread desire for simply withdrawing from such bases, even if it meant weakening the commitments that such bases supported. Especially if the nuclear attack had not yet been directed against such American forward units but had been accompanied by implicit or explicit threats that these units would be the *next* target, a certain slice of American opinion might be inclined to what would seem like withdrawal under threat of fire.

If such an American base had actually been the target of the initial nuclear escalation, the same inclination to withdraw might show up, but there would also be a strong desire for retaliation and revenge, which might then even enhance the forward deployments, and enhance the investments in TMD, rather than supporting a withdrawal.

In any event, those favoring a deemphasis of aircraft carriers and forward bases in face of the nuclear escalation threat would hardly all be inclined to reducing American involvement abroad. American professional military plan-

ners, and the American public at large, might at the same time favor investment in longer-range systems for conventional and other kinds of warfare,
systems that might be based more securely back in the United States, perhaps
behind a national missile defense shield, able then to execute many of the
missions that might previously have been carried out from the base on Diego
Garcia or Guam.[10]

It is difficult to imagine any new use of nuclear weapons that would not
capture the attention of every person who was at all concerned with international affairs. The benchmark for comparison again might be whether
everyone afterwards remembered where they were when they heard the news
of the event, as with the news of September 11, 2001. Yet it might be useful
to calibrate the salience of a nuclear escalation by looking at what might be
the *least* noticeable of such events. Leave aside acts conducted so discreetly
or subtly that there was a general uncertainty about whether a nuclear detonation was even involved, as perhaps with the use of a nuclear depth charge
deep in the ocean in the pursuit of some submarine. Rather we are asking
whether the world could find unstartling any clear and explicit detonation
of a nuclear weapon.

As noted, if the nuclear escalation occurred in the midst of a war that had
already seen great numbers of soldiers and civilians killed in conventional
combat, or if it occurred in the context of a horrible use of biological or chemical weapons, the shock of the *nuclear* event would assuredly be less. If the use
came when major famines or natural diseases were already killing tremendous
numbers of people, the shock of a use would similarly be less.[11]

One must also note the unevenness in how public opinion identifies with
human life and human suffering around the globe; there is some elementary
racism everywhere by which people identify more with the happiness or suffering of people who resemble themselves and less with those who seem somehow very different.

Putting together these considerations, as we search for a scenario where the
use of nuclear weapons did not immediately shock Americans, one might suggest the introduction of such weapons into one of the wars that have been
raging in Central Africa, amid the tremendous ambient suffering already produced by conventional munitions, the resulting disruption of the economy,
and by the enormous tragedy of the AIDS epidemic. Japanese and European
and American opinion might be very disturbed to hear that a nuclear weapon,
somehow smuggled into the combat, had been used in Africa, and the gov-

ernments of the democracies might feel that they had to contemplate major changes in policy; but the urgency and impact might well seem more minor than the destruction of a city or military base of a major power.

Less Defeatist Responses to a Rogue State Attack (Category E)

The American public has generally responded with overwhelmed surrender to the AIDS epidemic in Africa, where the numbers of projected victims are so horrible that most of us slip into a sort of denial, reinforced by a feeling that nothing can be done to alleviate the epidemic. Where the feeling is instead that something *can* be done, the American people tend toward assertiveness. In response to a nuclear escalation, they might well favor policies of preemption and punishment, up to and including the utilization of American nuclear weapons. The difference between the American reactions to AIDS and to anthrax attacks is instructive here. The latter disease has done far less damage to Americans, but its appearance in letters to congressmen was correctly viewed as a deliberate attack on the United States by a conscious adversary, someone who needed to be identified and punished, someone who needed to be physically prevented from repeating these attacks. The mere fact that something *can be done* about a situation dwarfs the degree of damage that the attacker is capable of inflicting.[12]

One should thus not underrate the strand of American response to a nuclear escalation that might push for major interventions, which might extend to the launching of preemptive and preventive wars. Where the example of a nuclear escalation was likely to produce further nuclear attack throughout a region, the response might well be that some of the perpetrator's nuclear arsenals should be destroyed, if their locations can be identified, perhaps even by the use of *American* nuclear weapons, before any more cities or bases are destroyed.

As noted, underestimation of the American willingness to persevere in a conflict and to seek revenge, the mistake that the Japanese made in 1941, led to the only use of nuclear weapons thus far in history. Especially if American ground or American forward bases had been hit, a great portion of the American public would be quite willing to risk further nuclear attacks in order to punish the launcher of the first attack. The persuasive arguments here would be that such an adversary could not be appeased and that, having inflicted this kind of damage on the United States once and having not been punished or eliminated from the scene, there would be no guarantee that he would not inflict such an attack again.

For all the reasons noted, many of the scenarios for nuclear escalation will thus tend to suggest a greater leaning toward American intervention in the conflict than any kind of withdrawal resembling 1920s isolationism. But rather than prompting a general unilateralism in American foreign policy, such a traumatic event might see more American utilization of the United Nations Security Council and General Assembly, as it would be important to muster as large a "posse" as could be collected, whether the United States is the principal victim of the original attack or merely the "sheriff" that takes the lead in responding to an attack on someone else.[13]

Aside from defending American national interests and commitments, however, Americans will be concerned that this nuclear warfare by a rogue state be brought to a halt as quickly as possible, and that the example be punished rather than accepted as a precedent for the future. As in anything, the strands of American interest in this can conflict with each other in complicated ways.

Two-Sided Nuclear Wars (Category F)

When confronting a nuclear exchange between two opposing powers, Americans' decisions might be driven by whether one side or the other had been a trusted friend and ally in the past; such considerations have always been important in any nation's response to a war. Or the American public's response might be driven by the logic of collective security, by which the most important question would be which side had initiated the war, with the victim to be defended and the conflict initiator punished.[14]

But, for most Americans, both of these considerations might well be overwhelmed by the sheer enormity of the destruction being inflicted, every time another foreign city was subjected to nuclear attack. If the sheer horror of this did not drive Americans to look away, it might induce them to favor urgent interventive action, placing termination of the nuclear war ahead of considerations of comparative guilt or previous friendship.

The Use of Established Nuclear Arsenals (Category G)

Americans have generally been less ready than other peoples (the West Europeans, for example) to accept the logic of "limited war." While European monarchs in earlier centuries often sent their armies forward for less-than-total causes, ordering their troops to be careful not to damage the province being conquered, American participation in wars has usually been of an all-or-nothing variety, amid talk of "Hang the Kaiser" and "unconditional surrender."[15] The logic by which the Korean War was limited (as all the other wars have since Stalin acquired a nuclear force, ending the American nuclear monopoly) has never been popular with the American people at large.[16]

If the next use of nuclear weapons were thus to be by a country whose nuclear arsenal was sizable, such that the United States could not simply go for unconditional surrender and total punishment of the guilty, there would be some Americans who would regard a "limited war" response as a craven surrender by their government, just as some accused Harry Truman of such surrender during the Korean War.[17]

One should thus not exaggerate the likelihood that the Russian or Chinese government, or any future government possessing a sizable nuclear arsenal, could get away with a "limited" introduction of nuclear weapons into some conflict. The risks of escalation to all-out nuclear war would remain, just as they did during the Cold War, making it dangerous for any country to try "limited nuclear war."[18]

But the United States, for the entire Cold War, had to overcome its characteristic distaste for having to fight with only some of its weapons, while having to hold others in reserve. The logic by which war has to be kept "limited" is unwelcome when one's young soldiers are being killed on "conventional" battlefields, but it may be unavoidable. In the Korean War and since then, subscribing to this logic has resulted in American nuclear weapons' being held in reserve, even when American soldiers were being attacked with conventional weapons. In our scenario here, the same logic might dictate that some or all of the American nuclear arsenal should be held in reserve, even when a portion of an adversary's nuclear arsenal had come into use.

Ultimately Ambiguous Cases

Always a little more complicated would be the American popular reaction if the first use of nuclear weapons was by a country which the United States regarded as a friend. Here, as noted, there would be less of the shock that stems from outrage, as many Americans would be quick to find reasonable explanations for why such an ally had felt itself forced to use nuclear weapons. If the use of nuclear weapons was in a largely countermilitary mode (for example, the use of a nuclear depth charge by the British Navy), there would be much less shock in general, of course, and more a perception of "business as usual." If the use involved a substantial destruction of civilian targets, there would be shock among Americans, but a shock mostly free of anger or any need for revenge. The instinct would be to help the victims while generally moderating the conflict that had brought on this use of nuclear weapons in the first place.

Much more complicated and less clear American popular reactions might emerge in scenarios that mix up the characteristics noted so far, events less at the center of nuclear escalation nightmares but where, for example, the side using nuclear weapons had good reason to do so, in American eyes, and was a friend or ally of the United States, or where no party claimed responsibility for a very destructive attack and the source of the weapon had not yet been determined. In such kinds of cases, the American reaction might be not so much shock as simple confusion; there would be confusion about whether or not to condemn the attack, about how to retaliate for it, and about what to do with the precedent that had just been set.

Most confusing of all for an American public would be if the first nuclear weapon used since Nagasaki had again been an *American* weapon. For all the years of the Cold War, an important ingredient of the American commitment to NATO and to South Korea included leaving open the possibility that American theater nuclear weapons might be used even if the opposing side had not used such weapons. Americans persisted in rejecting the "no-first-use" proposals put forward by Moscow, regarding them as a political trap, as a way of "making Europe safe for conventional war." The United States and NATO have to this date still not terminated the declared policies of "flexible response," policies which include some risk that, if defenses were otherwise failing, the United States would initiate the use of nuclear weapons.[19]

Attitudes on Intervention

At the minimum, a use of nuclear weapons anywhere around the world is likely to change American criteria for intervention.[20] In the absence of such a nuclear escalation, much of the American public debate on intervention has been phrased in terms of whether becoming involved in a given conflict is worth risking the lives of American soldiers, be it to prevent ethnic massacres in some "failed state" in Africa or Eastern Europe or to prevent famines somewhere else. After a nuclear weapons use, one would anticipate a greater American willingness to risk conventional casualties and to pay the material costs of maintaining and deploying conventional forces.

Once again, the outrageous events of September 11, 2001, offer a clue to the differences expected here. Even if the United States had not itself been the immediate victim, if Islamic terrorists had instead seized airliners to smash into high-rise buildings in London or in Tel Aviv or even in Moscow, the arguments for unilateralism would have seemed weaker, and the arguments for an American coordination with like-minded powers would have been stronger. Just as Britain volunteered its conventional forces to join in the military effort responding to the September 11 attack, Americans might have felt it appropriate to commit forces if that attack had been on London.

Aside from taking action against the perpetrator of a nuclear attack, Americans would follow another instinct they have demonstrated over history, that is, to relieve the suffering of victims of attack, to offer aid to the wounded and displaced, to help rebuild structures that were destroyed. This instinct might hold even if no American assets had been damaged in the original attack, even if the use of nuclear weapons had come in an exchange in which the United States was not identified with either side. Thus, one implication of a next use of nuclear weapons would be that the logistics resources of the U.S. military would have to be prepared for an enormous task of delivering medical and other relief aid to the regions that had been struck; regardless of whether the American people chose to intervene in any other way, the enormity of the human suffering involved and the urgency of offering some remedy would probably dictate this.

Attitudes on Arms and Arms Control

As noted for the world as a whole, the use of a nuclear warhead would change American attitudes on arms control and on weapons procurement. One might envisage a resumption of nuclear testing, designed to tailor new nuclear warheads, perhaps of much smaller yields, so that the "graduated nuclear attacks" of an adversary could be responded to at the appropriate level; in the horror of seeing a nuclear warhead used anywhere in the world against a *real* target, the world's aversion to the possible radioactive fall-out released in a *test* detonation would be immediately less, and the practical arguments in favor of testing would seem enhanced.

At the level of strategic reasoning, if someone else had already used nuclear weapons, if Americans or someone else had already suffered the devastation of such an attack, there would be less reluctance among Americans about launching *nuclear* counterattacks, at the minimum at the same destructive level as the original attack.

Similarly, the horror of a *nuclear* attack would, relatively speaking, reduce somewhat the horror Americans felt at the idea of a chemical or biological attack. In the aftermath of the September 11 terrorist attacks and the subsequent mailings of anthrax spores, the United States is tightening up its defenses against biological and chemical weapons. In the general toughening up (as previously hypothetical threats become much more real), Americans may consider whether it might be wise to reacquire offensive chemical and biological weapons, which would round out the American ability to practice "graduated deterrence," that is, to retaliate in kind, to hit back at the same level that the adversary had initiated.[21]

There are people in the United States and around the world who regard it as illogical and morally inconsistent for the United States to wish to retain nuclear weapons when other states are asked to forego acquiring them, and for the United States perhaps even to augment its nuclear arsenal and its conventional arsenal while preaching nonproliferation.[22] Yet one does not have to be very much of a "realist" to note that the decision-making processes of interacting states are often prone to such moral inconsistency. Others argue that for the United States to equip itself for "escalation dominance" and "graduated deterrence," so that it can respond at just the right level to anyone else's use of nuclear or other weapons of mass destruction (applying appropriate punishment while always holding some additional punishment in reserve), will actually work to *discourage* proliferation, much more than encouraging it by some kind of moral affront. The logic is to convince nations that they cannot further their interests by using nuclear weapons, or even by acquiring such weapons, since the United States can always beat them in this suit.[23]

It is important to note that the very best service of global goals would be if the United States never actually had to use any of its own nuclear weapons, just as the most effective police force may be one that never has to fire its handguns. But a police force that did not even possess any guns with which to shoot would not discourage criminality. The nuclear weapons of the American arsenal may have to be maintained in a variety of sizes if nuclear peace is to be maintained.

It certainly is also plausible that any use of nuclear weapons around the globe would make Americans more supportive of investment in national missile defenses. Even if one also had to worry about other ways that nuclear weapons could be delivered to American soil, it would seem appropriate to try to block *all* avenues of attack. One would also see a renewed interest in civil defense preparations and in a resurrection of the air defenses needed to stop a bomber attack or delivery of a nuclear weapon by a cargo aircraft.[24]

Actions taken after the September 11 terrorism suggest the likelihood of these responses. Resources were allocated to maintaining interceptor patrols above American cities to, if necessary, shoot down any highjacked airliner that seemed bound for use as a missile to destroy a major building. The concern about the anthrax attacks and other possibilities of chemical and biological terrorism similarly have reinvigorated the civil defense planning that many Americans, after the success of the Cold War reasoning of mutual assured destruction, had stopped thinking about.

Constraints on Civil Liberties

Similarly foreshadowed by U.S. actions in the wake of the September 11th attacks is a demand for tighter border controls, so that weapons of mass destruction cannot be smuggled into the United States by automobile or in suitcases, and a demand for much tighter identity controls, not only for aliens visiting the United States, but perhaps for American citizens as well, which civil libertarians see as a major first step toward threatening the freedoms Americans hold dear.

Especially if an American city or an American base abroad were destroyed in the first nuclear attack and if the nuclear attack were by terrorists with no foreign government identification, the American public might demand much more stringent compromises of traditional civil liberties, on the argument that the nuclear factor had put so many more lives at risk, and that this higher level of risk would need to be balanced against preservation of normal freedoms.[25]

In the immediate aftermath, the attacks of September 11th were often likened to the Pearl Harbor attack, as members of Congress and others compared the surprise factor in these two assaults on American soil. But our worst memories of Pearl Harbor are mingled with a guilt about the ways in which Japanese-Americans were treated, and thus far nothing as bad has occurred toward most Arab-Americans or toward Muslims in general.

When the nuclear factor is added to the picture, however, more extreme popular reactions might show up, some of them quite horrible to contemplate, for example, a popular tolerance for torturing the suspected conspirators in any such nuclear terrorism. What a nuclear attack on an American city would do to American standards of civil liberty may indeed be one of the more worrisome impacts we have to consider.

American Reactions Overall

In the course of this exercise in speculating about the *likely* American reactions to nuclear escalation we have sampled all the major scenario categories.

There are many levels on which the situation would seem beset with ambiguities and confusion. There are cases imaginable in which the nuclear escalation would not seem so very destructive and ones that were accidents.

If *mass* destruction were indeed the effect, the American public might fall into a panicked flight from the world, with sizable numbers calling for a withdrawal from any commitments that might draw nuclear attack upon the United States, this being in effect a policy of preemptive surrender. For the reasons cited, this panic has to be rated as possible, but as not the most likely response. Yet a serious risk remains that a foreign power or a non-state terrorist actor might overrate the likelihood of this kind of response, even though such a projection is not supported by the American response to Pearl Harbor or the responses to the invasions of South Korea or Kuwait, and it is not supported by the American response to the attacks on the Pentagon and the World Trade Center. One strand of historical experience that might support an expectation of American withdrawal is the popular reaction against the casualties suffered in the Vietnam War.[26]

More likely is a very militant American response to a nuclear escalation, a response focused on retaliation and on the preemption of future attacks. For the escalation scenarios that most often come to mind, a use of nuclear weapons against America or its allies with attacks on civilians, this American response would lead to an open-ended conflict, until the perpetrator of the original nuclear attack was brought to justice or destroyed as a military force.

But against an adversary that had been prudent enough to acquire a number of nuclear weapons, so that it was not engaging in "unilateral nuclear disarmament" in its first strike, a more troublesome course of *limited* American responses might be an unavoidable necessity, even if it is a course that would be difficult for many Americans to swallow.

CHAPTER FIVE

Appropriate United States Policy Responses

Having outlined a wide range of ways that nuclear weapons could again come into use, a variety of global popular and governmental reactions, and likely American popular reactions, we now suggest *appropriate* United States policy responses to the scenarios we have described. The discussion will begin with some general observations about what we would hope to see here.

The damage of such a nuclear escalation will be less, and the possible *gains* greater, if there has been advance planning for the various ways in which such an event could occur, rather than having the United States government caught by surprise and then react on an ad hoc basis. To repeat a caveat noted at the outset, anticipating such an occurrence does *not* have to mean that we are pessimistically resigned to expecting future nuclear weapons use or are in any way welcoming it. Rather, preparation indicates that some prior thought has been given to the policy choices and likely consequences.

All "war plans" and other advance planning for policy contingencies have definite limitations. They remain based in speculation; if one convinces oneself that one has seen the future in such a planning exercise, one risks being caught even more by surprise if an actual event deviates from the anticipated scenario.

Yet a decision to avoid any advance consideration of the likely forms of nuclear weapons use, for fear of being accused of excessive pessimism or for fear of creating a self-confirming hypothesis, would sacrifice opportunities to minimize the losses after a nuclear attack, and opportunities for such an event to make American policy more effective in the future.

Even disasters may contain opportunities, which are put to best use if they are recognized early. And it may be that not every use of nuclear weapons will amount to a disaster, for the world or for the United States.

United States Preeminence

It is likely that the United States will remain the preeminent power in the world, in economic strength and conventional military capabilities as well as in the size and qualities of its nuclear arsenal, into the foreseeable future.[1] This has some enormous benefits for the United States and the world, since most of the world has had reason to see America as a very benevolent leader, a force whose presence tends to maintain peace rather than disturb it, a force for prosperity around the world.[2] Yet there are individuals and governments that resent this American preeminence and insist on portraying the United States as a nonbenevolent "hegemon," rather than as a helpful leader. There are also, indeed, many Americans who do not relish the role of being a hegemon or "world policeman" in the post–Cold War world. The risk of America's being the target of the first new use of nuclear weapons, or in the *next* use after that, are increased by its visibility and preeminence, because what would drive the targeting of nuclear escalation is likely to be not the world's interest but the deep resentments of some national or terrorist leader.

One major generic question affecting reactions to nuclear escalation thus is whether the United States will seek to maintain its preeminent status, in the military and other fields, or to reduce it, letting other powers become more central to the maintenance of world law and order and prosperity. And the other generic question of course is whether the world is willing to be led by the United States.

In considering the world's acceptance of an American leadership role, one could compare the international response to Saddam Hussein's 1990 invasion of Kuwait, which very much illustrated the American role of a "sheriff" recruiting a "posse," with the much lower support and enthusiasm displayed in the response to Saddam Hussein's 2003 failure to comply with all the conditions of the earlier truce (most especially the acceptance of reliable safeguards that he was not producing weapons of mass destruction).[3] Perhaps the difference in response is explained by the difference in stimulus; the earlier aggression was so blatant, while the latter failure to cooperate with inspectors was more debatable. Or perhaps the outside world had simply become more fatigued and less resolute as the years had passed, while the Clinton administration succeeded that of the senior President Bush, only to be succeeded itself by the younger President Bush.

Yet, the case we are contemplating here, of an actual *use* of nuclear weapons, would most probably be even more blatant than a transboundary conventional aggression, and thus more likely again to reinforce the American leadership role.

This American leadership role has always been acknowledged only quietly by most countries. The United States has informally become a sort of "sheriff" for the maintenance of world peace, such that countries like Singapore welcome the presence of the United States Navy off their coasts. The responses of the United States to any aggression were expected to be in tune with the interests of the entire world (certainly more so than would be the responses of any other power one might name). Rather than having "vigilante" action by other powers, most of the world welcomed the responses of the United States, at least for as long as Washington showed a willingness to consult with others about possible courses of action, and for as long as America showed itself to be free of the kinds of selfish imperialist motives that drove earlier hegemons.[4]

Some Americans, and some foreign commentators, have been calling for the United States to revert to the role of "ordinary country," rather than being "world policeman," "sheriff," or hegemon. For many reasons, however, the United States is almost predestined to be the world leader, given the role of the dollar as the world's currency and English as the world's language, the preeminence of America's universities, and the strength of its armed forces. A nuclear escalation might demonstrate the dangers of this preeminence, but it might just as well prove to be an illustration of why this preeminence has to be maintained and brought to bear.

Threats to American Sovereignty?

Apart from the debate about whether the United States should be the sheriff of the post–Cold War world (a debate which would be very much brought to life by a nuclear weapons use anywhere in the world) or should instead retreat to the role of an ordinary country, there will be Americans who fear that the United States, in the face of cataclysmic world events, might lose the prerogatives of even an ordinary country.[5] Rather than envisaging nuclear escalation as an opportunity for the United States to challenge the sovereignty of other states on behalf of world law and order, such people would be fearful instead of challenges to American sovereignty, as new principles of international law were conjured up to limit the options that the United States previously held for its own foreign policy.

This fear might, of course, come closest to being realized if it were the United States that first used nuclear weapons again, especially if the circumstances surrounding the use were not such as to win widespread international understanding for the act. But, regardless of which country was first to use nuclear weapons, there might be a groundswell of world public opinion and governmental policies directed toward making further use of *any* weapon of mass destruction "illegal" in the future, perhaps simply making it a "war crime," to be tried at The Hague (this being the worst fear of those Americans who worry that a new international standard for war crimes might override the United States Constitution and the normal prerogatives of sovereignty).[6]

Even were the launcher of nuclear escalation a clear enemy of the United States, a country as internationally obnoxious as North Korea, there would thus be some American caution about carving out grand new precedents of higher international law, lest such precedents soon enough be turned against the United States.

New principles of international law might indeed be established after the disaster of a nuclear weapon's being used to destroy a city. But many of us might advocate letting these principles be carved out by something more positive, by the spread of stable democracy and domestic rule of law to a great many more countries, so that their instinct for the preservation of individual liberties and restraint of government would be as well developed as it is in the United States. Until then, many Americans will retreat into a strong defense of sovereignty, of the separateness of American political processes, even if this limits how much new "international law" can be generated in response to a nuclear escalation.

One possible consequence of a use of nuclear weapons might thus be that American opinion, and world opinion, would push the United States government, against its will and against the important strategic goals that have held for decades of American defense policy, into accepting the constraints of a policy of no first use of nuclear weapons. This would not be a trivial development.[7]

The skeptics about such a pledge, issued so often by China since 1964 and by the Soviet Union in its last years (to be rescinded now), sometimes compare it to the Kellogg-Briand pact renouncing war at the end of the 1920s. It is always possible that a country possessing nuclear weapons would not abide by its pledge of never using them until another country had used them first, but the pledges made by a democracy are different from those made by a cynical dictatorship. The important point about nuclear first use was always that it took a fair amount of effort to make such escalation credible and plausible in the first place, escalation on behalf of an ally threatened with being overrun by an attacker's conventional forces.

There will always be circumstances in which a country that had committed itself to no first use of nuclear weapons might renege on its pledge, for example if the country were about to be overrun by a conquering army, such that the regime had nothing left to lose. But the likely situations for American first use or renunciation of first use would be the cases calling for *extended* nuclear deterrence, for declarations and treaties and force deployments designed to make American nuclear escalation on behalf of some threatened ally credible, where it otherwise would not be credible.[8]

If the United States, after the horror of a nuclear attack somewhere around the globe, were driven by world opinion or American voter opinion to declare that it would not use nuclear weapons against an opponent who had not used them first, such a shift in American declaratory policy would reduce or eliminate the deterrent coverage that shielded NATO and South Korea against conventional attack for the decades of the Cold War. The United States could always use nuclear weapons even when it had promised not to; the "realists" and cynics about the power of international commitments would be correct that a pledge that is not enforceable by higher authority will not have the equivalent strength of domestic law. But, a no-first-use pledge would greatly diminish the deterrent impact of the prospect of nuclear escalation.

We considered above, and largely dismissed, the possibility that the next use of nuclear weapons would produce a horror and revulsion leading to global nuclear disarmament. The inherent difficulties of verification almost surely indicate that such disarmament will not happen. But the elimination of the American freedom to threaten the first use of such weapons is a more likely possibility, not necessarily negated or made meaningless by any inherent difficulties of verification.

American forswearing of nuclear escalation threats would be most likely if a city had been destroyed, of course, as compared with the scenarios where the nuclear attack had caused little collateral damage. Attempts to obtain commitments of American restraint might be even more likely if the use of nuclear weapons had been by *American* forces, especially if the world had not seen any great need or justification for such an escalation. If the introduction of nuclear weapons did not actually serve any military purpose, did not succeed in repulsing some aggression, but merely increased the total of death and destruction, the world's prejudices against such weapons and against their use would be very much renewed.

For all the reasons cited, a no-first-use pledge by the United States would be a setback for American foreign policy, since a significant part of the security reassurances the United States offers its allies will still depend on keeping open and credible the possibility that American nuclear weapons would be used before any other power had done so. The credibility of American first use of nuclear weapons (often described as the American "nuclear umbrella") has played a major role in keeping West Germany and South Korea from reaching for nuclear weapons of their own, and it has played a major role in lowering the likelihood of conventional wars when major conventional forces faced each other in what would otherwise have been very dangerous and unstable confrontations.[9]

Those advocating a reduced reliance on nuclear weapons have often assumed that all their goals were compatible, that reducing any brandishing of American nuclear weapons would reduce the likelihood that nuclear weapons would spread into the possession of other countries. In countries like West Germany and South Korea, the impact of American self-restraint would have been just the opposite; and there will be countries in the future that will similarly be choosing between relying on American extended nuclear deterrence (which a declaration of no first use would negate) and acquiring their own nuclear weapons.

Ambiguity about Whether the Line Was Crossed (Category A)

If it were not certain that the nuclear taboo had been violated, because the facts were unclear about what had happened or because the definition of our crucial distinction was less than clear, the American national interest might dictate that the world be allowed to believe that nothing different had happened. Much of what goes on in this world is a function of what the world *thinks* has been going on, and any precedent for nuclear escalation would pose a great many risks of disaster for the future.

An example of such a case might be if a nuclear attack were blunted by someone's air defense or missile defense system, then rumors abounded that a nuclear warhead had been destroyed en route to its target, but the launcher of the attack and the interceptor stood ready to deny this or pretend that it could not be confirmed.

Similarly, a conventional attack against a nuclear power reactor or against a smaller reactor dedicated to the production of fissionable material might be defined as nuclear escalation, or it might not, depending on how the U.S. government, and the world, chose to label it. If the attack did not threaten the lives of large numbers of people, there might be advantages to maintaining the image of an unviolated taboo.

Another ambiguous case, noted at the outset, would be a nuclear test during a major crisis or during an ongoing war, with the whole world assuming that the test detonation was intended to intimidate the adversary of the moment. There were such uses of nuclear testing during the Cold War, to show resolve in the ongoing confrontation between the United States and the Soviet Union;[10] and the Indian and Pakistani "tests" of 1998 were surely intended to send political signals of toughness at least as much as they were designed to resolve any uncertainties about the technologies of the weapons involved.[11] These "tests" were thus "a use of nuclear weapons" just as such weapons were "used" in a declaratory mode for decade after decade for the purposes of deterrence; but the world's taboo on nuclear attacks was not regarded as violated or contradicted by these test detonations, for people have fastened on the destruction of a city or of some other target as the definition of violation, rather than on the mere brandishing of the potential for such an attack.

Even closer to the line we are debating here would be a "demonstration shot," by which a nuclear weapon was detonated in such fashion as not to do any immediate physical damage, perhaps high in the atmosphere but nevertheless in the airspace of the opposing side, in a clear violation of that state's sovereignty.[12] In an ongoing war, this would be a signal that the *next* nuclear warhead detonated would indeed do damage, but much of the world might see even such a preliminary demonstration use of a nuclear weapon as a violation of the taboo.

The closer one gets to the borderlines of the conceptual definitions of a use of nuclear weapons the more difficult it becomes to predict whether the world will be inclined to write off such an event and define it away as not quite a "use in anger" of such weapons, and the more difficult it may therefore be for the governments of the world's democracies to implement any policy that would define away such marginal cases.

It must be stressed that attempting in such cases to convince the world that the taboo had not been violated would not be a policy of just sticking one's head in the sand, of avoiding unpleasantness rather than facing it. It would, rather, be a policy of avoiding the self-confirming cycles of pessimism by which a marginal and debatable violation of the prior patterns of restraint might lead everyone to assume that all such restraint had been terminated.

The non-use of nuclear weapons in attacks on cities and opposing territory is, in the net, a pattern that the democracies and the entire world will benefit from extending. It has been extended thus far in part because patterns of behavior, good and bad, tend to renew themselves, because the countries of the world tend to think twice before embarking on the kind of attack that hit Japan in 1945, an attack that has not been repeated since. To label any particular attack as the "next nuclear strike after Nagasaki" should thus be a major decision, not the unanalytical act of local newscasters; to avoid the application of the label, where the facts allow that such a depiction of events can reasonably be avoided, might be to head off bigger disasters in the future.

One could move the level of scenario up a notch and consider a preemptive attempt to eliminate the nuclear arsenal of a state that seemed to be falling apart. If India decided that this was the situation in Pakistan (India perhaps indeed *wanting* Pakistan to fall apart, much as the United States in many ways welcomed the dissolution of the Soviet Union), and if India then launched conventional air strikes and/or commando raids to destroy or seize the Pakistani nuclear arsenal, this might rest just at the edge of our range of nuclear scenarios (it would certainly capture the attention of the United States government as much as an outright use of nuclear weapons in anger). It is hardly beyond imagination that the United States or its closer allies might one day be in the situation outlined hypothetically here for India against Pakistan, wherein the nuclear weapons stockpile of a collapsing regime, perhaps in North Korea, would be preemptively destroyed to keep it from coming into use.

Such an outside attempt to eliminate an existing nuclear arsenal might be accompanied by another marginal and ambiguous case, an unsuccessful attempt by the collapsing state to launch one of its nuclear weapons in a strike at the outside world.

The range of policy choices in the face of such ambiguous situations thus includes everything from cosmetic coverup to active intervention. By the very nature of the ambiguity factor here, there is a greater risk that the United States would be caught by surprise and hence be uncertain of what to do. To repeat, a critic might see the suggested policy option of pretending that nothing different had happened as a simple evasion, as a turning off of the alarm clock bell, as a weak and unprepared reaction to being caught by surprise. But where the situation is truly more marginal, there may be a well-thought-out case for not having alarm bells ringing all around the world.

There is, thus, a strong argument to be made for prolonging the time over which the world senses that nuclear weapons have not been used. An extension of the *apparent* taboo would work to reinforce the taboo and to reduce the chances that powers all around the world would then see it as appropriate to acquire and use nuclear weapons. If an event is in the gray zone of how "nuclear escalation" is defined, the national interests of the United States might well be served by supporting any tendency in world opinion to treat a marginal case as a nonviolation, as something *other* than the first use of a nuclear weapon since Nagasaki.

As a matter of policy, this could not *always* be the recommendation. An attempt to maintain a useful fiction could collapse badly if rumors continued to emerge, if more and more facts came out after a time, and if the participation of the United States government in what had been a cosmetic coverup then made the world's eventual shock even greater.

But rumors often fade if not definitively confirmed, and without producing a major shock to the system, as the world moves ahead, sticking to a more reasonable pattern of conduct despite reports that one party or another has deviated from it.

A related policy line would be that the United States try to anticipate the wide variety of such possibly ambiguous cases, ranging from conventional attacks on nuclear power plants to the spreading of nuclear garbage (all the cases noted at the outset, and possibly a good many others), with a view to having an American response ready for each of such borderline cases, a response outlining why one scenario is to be treated as a nuclear escalation and another is not. To repeat a general point, the less the United States is surprised by any particular event, the better it will be equipped to keep the world from being shocked by such an event, shocked in a way that might lead to repeated uses of nuclear weapons. A sorting of the possibly ambiguous cases would then be matched with a set of "talking points" for each, a plan for how the United States would try to lead the world in interpreting each case.

Cases with Surprisingly Low Collateral Damage (Category B)

We turn now to the second range of scenarios that has been outlined, cases in which nuclear weapons have definitely been used, by any definition and by all observer accounts, but the nuclear attack has been very much limited, so that far fewer people have been killed than at Hiroshima and Nagasaki (perhaps no one at all) and other considerations intervene to make the "news" of a violation of the nuclear taboo seem like "surprisingly good news." This again is a version of "surprise" for which Americans and others could be better prepared than they are today.

Under *some* of such circumstances, the wisest American policy may well be to accept and co-opt the precedent that has just been set of nuclear first use, much as it managed (without any actual occurrence of such use) to keep the first-use-threat deterrent alive for the protection of NATO and South Korea all through the decades of the Cold War. One would obviously not want a precedent that made *all* uses of nuclear weapons more acceptable and likely, but if the actual event had been in the benign category and had served a benign political purpose, a major effort might have to be made to dignify and clarify the event, rather than going along with any inclination to punish the escalation.

The above suggestion will shock some readers. For many analysts, the first U.S. reaction after *any* violation of the nuclear taboo should be to apply a maximum effort toward restoring the taboo. They reason that if the world sees such a nuclear escalation as having been made ineffective and having brought substantial and meaningful punishment down on the perpetrator, the lesson would be that this is an act not to be repeated, that the taboo or principle of international conduct has been reestablished. Rather than being followed by many repetitions, this use of nuclear weapons would come to be seen as the exception that proved the rule.

Yet one must keep in mind the subset of cases in which the United States would instead want to dignify a new status quo rather than seeing the return of a blanket taboo on nuclear weapons use, a new status quo wherein *some kinds* of nuclear use are regarded as more acceptable and normal. This could be the appropriate American response if the use of nuclear weapons was part of a defense against a massive conventional attack that could not otherwise have been repulsed, or if the use were by an ally of the United States or another democracy, or if the nuclear escalation had been carefully designed to avoid major civilian casualties, or if the use had come in response to someone else's use of other weapons of mass destruction, chemical or biological. Indeed, if anyone were seeking the perfect combination of circumstances to make a use of nuclear weapons acceptable, to avoid American or world condemnation of such use, and perhaps to erode the general taboo, the above would be the list of ingredients.

Looking at this list, one might note that these conditions comprised the scenarios of an *American* first use of nuclear weapons considered most plausible through the decades of the Cold War, when it was American national policy, for very sound reasons, to avoid becoming trapped in a no-first-use declaration and when, indeed, the most plausible introducer of nuclear weapons would have been the United States.

With the collapse of the Warsaw Pact and the Soviet Union, one often hears the comment that any American interest in extended nuclear deterrence must now have disappeared, as it is the Russians that today are talking about "flexible response," while the United States and its allies are credited with enormous advantages in conventional force capabilities.[13]

Yet the advantage in conventional warfare has sometimes been very transitory and unpredictable, and it could be quite premature to conclude that the United States and its allies will have lost all interest in exploiting the extended-deterrence aspect of nuclear weapons. The forces that had such an easy time rolling back the Iraqi invasion of Kuwait were basically the by-product of NATO's preparations for war with the Soviet Union, that is, a by-product of the Cold War, and these forces have been reduced in size in the decade since.

We must ask: Have all the older arguments for retaining *threats* of nuclear escalation really been overtaken by events? Are some of these arguments for extended nuclear deterrence still quite relevant? The blanket nuclear taboo was actually a nuisance for American policy all through the Cold War. The end of that conflict has definitely reduced the American reliance on credible threats of nuclear escalation in face of adversarial conventional forces, but it has not totally eliminated such reliance.[14]

Similarly, as the United States today faces the problem of how to deter an adversary's use of chemical and biological weapons, it is boxed in by its own decision three decades ago to forswear the mere possession of these types of weapons.[15] (A policy of no first use of chemical and biological weapons would have no logic to it when one has no such weapons to use, for there is no "tit-for-tat" retaliation with which to threaten the states that *do* possess such weapons.)

The argument is sometimes made that the robust American advantage in conventional weapons will supply the counter with which to punish an adversarial use of chemical or biological weapons. But what if such conventional weapons are already being used to the maximum of their potential in response to someone else's conventional aggression? The essence of deterrence is that one has to brandish something *additional* that has as yet been held in reserve, something that could be brought into play in response to the other side's new round of escalation.[16]

Many American analysts have therefore concluded that the only appropriate response to an adversary's introduction of chemical and biological weapons of mass destruction would be nuclear WMD. This line of reasoning lumps all weapons of mass destruction into a new *single* category regarding mutual deterrence and taboo. One of our scenarios for a first use of nuclear weapons could thus easily enough entail such action by the United States or by some other democratic government, possibly a government that had also renounced chemical and biological weapons when it was thought that this would set the worthwhile example by which all countries would renounce such weapons, a prediction that turned out to be badly founded.

To deter the use of chemical and biological WMD, the United States may wish to maintain the possibility of a first use of *nuclear* WMD. If such a use-in-response actually occurs, the United States may well *not* want to condemn it or erase the precedent but rather establish the example for its deterrent effect in the future.[17]

The lumping together of chemical, biological, and nuclear weapons as "weapons of mass destruction" thus has some advantages, but it also has disadvantages.[18]

For anyone advocating disarmament in general and renunciations of weapons use in general, such a redefinition might at first glance be viewed as a positive step, as more weapons would seemingly be brought under the ban.

On reflection, however, one quickly sees that this is a thinning out of the ban on nuclear weapons use. Rather than reserving nuclear weapons for use *only if* someone else uses *nuclear* weapons first, the new policy would accept their use if someone else launches a chemical or biological attack first.

On the positive side, an inclusive definition of WMD helps alert governments and peoples around the world that there are other weapons besides nuclear ones for which proliferation is to be avoided and for which a policy of non-use is to be encouraged. On the negative side, lumping them all together may diminish the priority assigned to the nonproliferation and non-use of nuclear weapons in particular.

It is important to note that nuclear weapons are still salient as compared to even the more frightening of the other destructive weapons, in how much death and destruction they can inflict, in the speed with which the destruction can be inflicted, and in how total and permanent the damage to the world would be.

The question has been asked, and will continue to be asked, as to why the taboo on the use of *nuclear* weapons in particular should be regarded as so special. The reactions of the world to the attacks on Hiroshima and Nagasaki and to the test detonations of thermonuclear weapons ever since Eniwetok suggest that ordinary people have come to see such weapons as different, as so destructive that they can never be treated as "just another weapon."

Another major disadvantage to lumping chemical and biological weapons together with nuclear weapons as weapons of mass destruction is that this might convey an impression to dangerous adversaries that they could rely on such other weapons as the functional equivalent, for deterrence purposes and other purposes, of nuclear weapons. To elevate the "poor man's H-bomb" to the status of actual nuclear weapons would perhaps be to convey that the United States and other sensible democracies are relatively easy to deter, even if acquiring nuclear weapons would have been too expensive for some potential "rogue state."

By the nature of its technological advantages, by the wording of the nuclear Nonproliferation Treaty, and by the history of the Cold War, the United States and Russia will hold a substantial advantage in nuclear weapons, an advantage that can be used to discourage the acquisition or use of nuclear weapons by more minor states. To equate the other kinds of WMD with nuclear weapons may be to sacrifice this advantage.

In light of the important arguments for retaining the plausible threat of nuclear escalation in the future, any *actual use* of nuclear weapons will jumble and confuse these *hypothetical* escalation threats, just as such an actual use would have done if it had occurred at any time during the Cold War. In the best of worlds, the actual use would serve as the perfect test case, demonstrating Western resolve, showing potential aggressors that they could not exploit any advantage they held in conventional weapons to get away with "limited war" conquests of territory. But in 2008 just as in 1958 or 1968, the actual use of nuclear weapons might not fit the dimensions of the perfect test case; and it might be necessary for the United States to mount a major effort to redefine actual use, so as to set the desired new precedent.

Looking at some applications of this policy that might have occurred in the past, such redefinition might have been the ideal policy if Britain had indeed used nuclear depth charges against an Argentine submarine during the Falklands War[19] or if Israel had used nuclear weapons against an Egyptian tank force in the Sinai Desert.[20] And this might automatically have been American policy if *American* forces had been driven to use nuclear weapons in some operation.

The world, because of the decades-long life of the nuclear taboo and the respect for the qualitative firebreak between conventional and nuclear weapons, would have been shocked and angered in any of these scenarios. Yet the shock would surely have been less than if a city had been hit or if a nondemocratic regime or a terrorist cell had been the launcher of the nuclear attack. The important point is that the United States might find it to its interest to avoid very large-scale reactions to, and condemnation of, such an instance of nuclear escalation.

Rather than pretending that nothing nuclear had happened here, the United States would instead have to be prepared to establish new firebreaks between acceptable and unacceptable introductions of nuclear weapons, so that the first use does not too much open the door for the second.

Again, the task may be one of sorting and identifying categories in advance, so that events do not arrive unanticipated. We may wish to have our arguments prepared as to why a specific kind of attack merits approval more than punishment.

But, burning in new firebreaks is not easy.[21] Careful thought will have to be given to whether any of the more benign precedents would boomerang against American interests: for example, if some adversary thus became free to fight "limited nuclear war" or if a particularly vicious dictatorship became freer to conduct nuclear war "in defense of" its continued existence as a regime. A speculative analysis must thus be undertaken, not just of the kinds of situations in which the United States might actually *welcome* someone's use of nuclear weapons, but of the kinds of bad follow-on precedent that might be set thereby. It would be a major accomplishment to design a way of seeing such cases as distinguishable from, and thus as decoupled as precedents from, the dangerous and undesirable follow-ons.

Irresponsible Nuclear Escalation (Category C)

Our third major category of scenarios comprises accidental or insubordinate launching of nuclear weapons, possibly involving outright insanity among the military officers or other people involved, with the governments who hold title to the nuclear warheads pleading, perhaps honestly, perhaps otherwise (with this always being difficult to tell), that they had not authorized such an attack.

One of the worst fears of Americans and others is indeed situations in which nuclear weapons are *out of control,* perhaps in the process of a crisis or war, because this makes all the mechanisms of deterrence as we know it much less reliable, and, no matter where the war is, puts American cities at risk.

As we speculate about the likelihood of a nuclear escalation, the portion of this total likelihood that would be assigned to an insane or otherwise irresponsible launching of an attack might have to be quite large, precisely *because* we all see the use of such weapons as so horrible. It is not quite the case that someone has to be crazy to use nuclear weapons, but if such a weapon is indeed used to destroy a city, the action might well not reflect any deliberate choice by a normal government.

It is also altogether possible, moreover, that a nuclear war, or even a war which was non-nuclear at the outset, could begin with tight command-and-control mechanisms, only to have these fall into disarray.[22] We noted above the case of an entire country falling apart under strains of confrontation from the outside world, the Soviet Union and Pakistan being two real-life examples. If a war is under way between two nuclear weapons states, much will depend on whether the first nuclear attacks are meant to destroy the opposing side's command-and-control structure, such as by targeting the national capital, or are instead carefully targeted away from this center of government, so as to maintain the possibilities of bargaining and truce.

Terrorists might well aim in particular at the national capitals of the governments they oppose. While it might have made no sense for the Soviet Union, in the Cold War scenarios of nuclear exchanges, to aim at Washington, it might make perfect sense for Al Qaeda, if it ever possessed a nuclear warhead, to try to destroy the American seat of government. Terrorists present multiple problems for the logic of deterrence. They have no country of their own at which retaliatory threats can be directed, and they have a vested interest in chaos generally. Where it might have been wise for Moscow to preserve Washington in the event of what we thought of as World War III, very different reasoning issues from someone like Osama bin Laden.

The reasoning by which the United States may have to intervene in someone else's nuclear war thus emerges. The highest priority may be to terminate the nuclear exchange, before punishment and retaliation get totally out of control. If the initial use of nuclear weapons was deliberate but was leading to a situation where the subsequent actions of either or both of the sides might be less deliberate, this might similarly require American intervention.

Especially if the use of nuclear weapons was the result of insubordination or accident, one clear policy thrust would be toward enhancements of command-and-control arrangements. There might be a great American willingness to share the techniques and equipment to bring this about.[23] Even where no obvious defect of such command systems had been involved in the first use of nuclear weapons, moreover, the subsequent increased tension and anticipation that someone else's weapons might be used would suggest that extra effort be devoted to avoiding the risks of accidental or unwanted nuclear strikes.

The United States would always want to discourage policies of "launch on warning," presumably even in today's dealings with Russia and China.[24] There would now be greater reason to fear self-confirming hypotheses; excessive anxiety in Pakistan about an Indian first strike could cause Pakistani nuclear weapons to be launched prematurely after an erroneous radar report. The antidotes to this situation are never easy to establish. They involve: a mixture of confidence-building arrangements sufficient to offer timely warning; the establishment of more-secure second-strike delivery systems, reducing fears of preemption; and the enhancement of command-and-control systems, to insure that a retaliatory strike can indeed be launched when needed but that it will *not* be launched when there is no need to retaliate.

Fostering these arrangements has been seen until now as "rewarding proliferation," allowing a country that had acquired nuclear weapons in defiance of United States and world opinion to replace its rudimentary and unstable weapons delivery systems with something much more robust. The United States and other states opposed to proliferation have thus always had a difficult choice, balancing the motives of these countries about nuclear weapons *proliferation* against the motives of the same countries about nuclear weapons *use*. The major point here is that a case of such *use* would give a higher priority to the prevention of *further* use, as compared with the still-important prevention of further proliferation. If an "nth" country defies the world's barriers to nuclear proliferation, the outside world will resent this but will at the same time want that country to have good command and control over its nuclear arsenal, lest the scenarios of nuclear insubordination, nuclear civil war, or nuclear terrorism be realized.

But, there are some inherent problems with a sharing of "permissive action links" (PAL) and other reinforcements for national command and control over nuclear weapons. For example, the governments that were offered such assistance might suspect that the United States would insert microchips into the locks and control systems that would give the United States a veto over the country's use of its own nuclear weapons.

Such suspicions might be less if the United States (or another long-time possessor of nuclear weapons) offered only advice, for instance, on how to screen the officers involved in the handling of such weapons, to weed out overly zealous officers who might have been perfect for ordinary combat but whose moderation and restraint might not be sufficient where so many thousands of lives are at stake.[25]

There is a clear moral hazard here, since all such assistance seems to reward proliferation and reduce the expectation of penalty for other states contemplating acquiring nuclear weapons. (We have heard such a policy labeled a "clean needles" approach, a reference to the difficult choices societies face in fighting drug addiction while also trying to mitigate the effects of such addiction.)

Helping a novice nuclear power control its new nuclear arsenal may thus get in the way of discouraging other countries from acquiring similar weapons. And the difficulties of choice apply even to the country that has already crossed the line, because enhancing its command-and-control arrangements, while desirable for some reasons, may allow it to move its nuclear weapons into more threatening deployments and enable it to be more venturesome in *expanding* its nuclear arsenal.[26]

Despite all these problems, there is nonetheless a powerful policy argument for the United States' quietly enhancing the national command authority of *any* country that has definitely acquired nuclear weapons, because the risk of such weapons' being used could thereby be substantially reduced. Appropriate planning would be to offer technological assistance that will not look suspicious to the receiving government and to take diplomatic actions that will reduce the visibility of such assistance.

The United States should also devote effort to enhancing its ability to identify the source of a nuclear weapon after any attack, for example, by the telltale isotope characteristics of its "nuclear fingerprint," so that the world would be able to attribute responsibility more reliably.[27]

If an actual detonation turned out to be the result of accident, insubordination, or craziness, additional advance thinking and planning would be desirable: How should such cases be punished? What compensation or responses will be demanded? To impose the same punishment that would result if the offending government had actually ordered the nuclear attack would *not* be sensible, for this would be to give that government no incentive to hold back the rest of its arsenal and no incentive to cooperate with the outside world in restoring control. But simply to shrug off the event and forgive the government whose nuclear weapons had been detonated irresponsibly would offend the moral sense of the world, and would similarly offer no incentive for a tightening of controls.

The point has to be stressed that this particular scenario of nuclear weapons use may have to be placed higher on the list of likelihoods precisely because *responsible* government decision making would have been deterred from any nuclear escalation. And a grim corollary is that terrorists and other weapons launchers separated from any government will be particularly dangerous to the United States, because of their incentive to try to destroy the entire American government.

Reactions to Mass Destruction: Preemptive Surrender? (Category D)

It is time now for us to return to what many readers will initially have seen as the *most* likely form of nuclear escalation, a nuclear attack deliberately launched by a government against a city, with a great many people being killed.

It was noted above that foreign publics and governments, and even portions of the American public, *might* be inclined to retreat in the face of such a use of nuclear weapons, endorsing demands that the United States withdraw its military forces and cancel its commitments in important areas around the world. For Americans, racing to appease the violator of the nuclear taboo might occur because U.S. cities had not yet been attacked and might be next or because an American city or military base had already been hit, thus suggesting what the full range of the disaster might become.

Most analysts of American foreign policy would regard such a retreat in face of the new nuclear threat as a political disaster, undermining the confidence other countries have had in American support and causing a fair number of such countries, Germany and Japan and others, to race to acquire their own nuclear warheads, in the medium-run thus actually *increasing* the risk that American cities will be destroyed.

As was demonstrated in the world's confrontations with Hitler and Mussolini and Stalin, it is extremely dangerous for a democratic government to advertise its fear of the worst a dictatorial and aggressive adversary can do, because this is taken as showing a lack of resolve that will embolden such adversaries to make new demands, and possibly launch new attacks.[28]

One of the more powerful arguments for a national system of missile defenses, augmented by a resuscitation of other air defense systems, and tighter border controls is that such defenses, even if imperfect, would likely stiffen the resolve of any American government facing new nuclear threats and would make that resolve more visible and persuasive to potential adversaries.[29]

No matter who the president of the United States was, increasing the chance that an attack launched against the United States itself could be blunted would make it easier for the president to intervene in response to a use of nuclear weapons elsewhere, rather than remaining aloof from the conflict.

One can outline a relatively short and limited list of situations in which the appropriate American policy would be to withdraw from the region where nuclear warfare had been initiated, to disassociate itself from such a region and its conflicts.

Such a situation might arise if the American people and government had a strong dislike for both sides in a conflict where nuclear weapons had been introduced, for example, the earlier rounds of warfare between Iran and Iraq. No responsible person in the United States would have *welcomed* a nuclear war between those countries, but there might have been relatively less regret, or urgency for intervention.

Even if there were no past grievances against the two sides, a similar policy, one of prudent neutrality, might develop, as the best reaction to a bad situation in which the American people and government had no great positive identification with either side. But, in today's increasingly inter-dependent world, such a situation is becoming hard to imagine. A "nuclear war" between Burma and Burundi might fit the model for American lack of identification, but it does not seem plausible that those countries would possess nuclear weapons; not every country in the world is acquiring the scientific wherewithal to produce nuclear weapons, and the United States has tended to be positively or negatively involved with all the current and likely possessors.

Of course, American identification is always somewhat influenced by the presence and activities of television reporters. Were Americans to see the aftermath of a nuclear attack, almost anywhere in the world, it would mobilize some strong sympathies, no matter who the people involved were.[30]

Another scenario, mentioned several times above, is if nuclear weapons were brought into use after a long and very damaging period of *conventional* warfare, with the nuclear escalation perhaps *ending* that war. In what would be a striking analogy to the one actual use of nuclear weapons in history, at Hiroshima and Nagasaki, this might produce sighs of relief rather than gasps of shock and might well steer American policy away from intervening.

Taking the opportunity to sever an alliance might be another reason for nonintervention. It is not easy to identify any American alliance commitments that one would *not* want to maintain after an attack, but historically, in the dynamics of competing national self-interests in the circles of power politics, there have been cases when a nation was seeking a way out of such commitments. Britain thus used the Washington Naval Disarmament Conference of 1921 as its excuse to terminate its formal alliance with Japan, and at the end of the eighteenth century the United States was seeking ways to terminate the alliance it had negotiated with France during the American War of Independence.[31] But the post–World War II alliances of the United States have been based on much more than considerations of power; in most cases, they have been derived from a real identification with the peoples and the political systems of the treaty partners.[32]

Where such was not the case, where a treaty commitment of the United States had somehow outlived its usefulness, it is imaginable, if not likely, that the American response to a nuclear escalation would be to terminate the treaty relationship rather than reinforce it by coming to the treaty partner's aid. A deliberate decision by the United States to retreat rather than to intervene in such a case might be appropriate if the American treaty partner was the state that had chosen to use nuclear weapons first and in a manner the U.S. government and people could not approve of. For an altogether hypothetical case, a sudden nuclear escalation by Pakistan in one of its crises and confrontations with India might cause the United States to declare its treaty bonds with Pakistan null and void. Thus, one form of punishment for such a violation of the nuclear taboo would be that a state lost its positive ties to the United States.

The only recent example of the United States' terminating a mutual-defense treaty with an ally was inspired by the opposite "nuclear" issue. In 1987 New Zealand declared a national policy that it would deny United States Navy ships entry to its ports unless there was an American assurance that such ships had no nuclear weapons on board. Since this requirement clearly conflicted with established American policy to "neither confirm nor deny" the presence of ship-borne nuclear warheads, the United States responded by terminating its mutual-defense treaty with New Zealand. One must note, however, that New Zealand faced no imminent threat of invasion by any hostile power; and even in the absence of a formal treaty commitment, the United States would hardly be likely to ignore such an invasion if it ever occurred.[33]

Anyone reading this study will most probably agree that an American withdrawal or surrender in face of a use of nuclear weapons is generally to be discouraged, because this would only bring more nuclear threats and actual uses of such weapons and would threaten all of what American foreign policy has stood for over the years since the bombing of Nagasaki. The point has been made above that the risk of such an American response is probably exaggerated, the real problem being that one foreign power or another may misread and underestimate the likely American resolve. Therefore, appropriate policy analysis must address how to bolster American resolve if there were any danger of its being lacking, and how to *clarify* and *communicate* such resolve to Pyongyang or Tehran or whatever regime might be the source of trouble.

Advocates of NMD and of other defenses for the homeland have made a strong case that such protection would increase American resolve on behalf of allies around the world and make that resolve more credible. But, just as during the Cold War, there has been a counterargument that our *seeking* such defenses might actually make us look less resolute, especially when such defenses might never be perfect. The mere fact that Americans were seeking defenses might suggest to a foreign dictator that the American government or people were very frightened by the prospect of a nuclear attack, so frightened that concessions could be extracted from the United States by threatening such an attack.[34]

Yet it is important to note that Americans have not shrunk from crises and challenges in the past, even when their country was wide open to the devastation that the Soviet Union could always have inflicted. And it would be important to study past examples of foreign decision makers' underrating American resolve, to look for ways of better advertising that resolve. The responses to the September 11th attacks, like the aftermaths of the earlier terrorist attempt to destroy the World Trade Center and the terrorist attacks on the American embassies in East Africa, were not illustrations of an American inclination to retreat.

Less Defeatist Responses to a Rogue State Attack (Category E)

Which potential American responses to a nuclear escalation would be appropriate depends a great deal on three factors: on whether the victim or perpetrator had been an ally of the United States, on who was to blame for the escalation and thus would have to be punished to maintain the proper precedent, and on whether there was an imminent risk of repetition of the nuclear attack. These considerations might interact in complicated and contradictory ways.

We naturally tend to begin any worried discussion of nuclear escalation with scenarios in which the launcher of nuclear warfare was not a friend or ally of the United States. If this nuclear attack were launched by a *nuclear novice,* a country with a very limited nuclear arsenal, and involved the killing of tens of thousands of people, the appropriate American policy, as seen by the American public and the world public, might have to be to go for "unconditional surrender," for a total disarmament of the culprit.[35]

Such a regime would, by its action, have eliminated any belief by the outside world that it could be trusted with the possession of weapons of mass destruction, or indeed perhaps any weapons at all. Such a regime would have put itself into the category of the Nazi regime in 1945 or the Taliban in 2001, a regime whose control over military forces and whose political power should be eliminated.

The prediction here is that such a view of things would emerge quite naturally around the world, as part of the shock at destruction of a city. Rather than having American policy planners work in advance to *design* how this kind of nuclear escalation must be punished, we instead suggest the policy task of being *ready* for such a world reaction, ready to shape and co-opt it as backing for a very strong American response.

Energetic responses to a violation of the nuclear taboo could take the form of a major expansion of what the world has come to see as the purview of international law. Just as some optimists about the growing international community have anticipated a new "customary international law" banning the use of nuclear weapons anywhere, the violation of this supposed ban might establish an international punishment for any such violation.

If the perpetrator of nuclear escalation was a dictatorial regime, this transgression might be viewed internationally as a reason to impose democracy on that country, to liberate the people from being governed without their consent, while presumably reducing the risk for other countries that such nuclear attacks would be repeated in the future.

Whether or not there was any expanded international law (which possibility liberals easily overrate but which "realists" sometimes underrate and dismiss too quickly), the precedent of a blatant introduction of nuclear weapons might also set the stage for some very helpful *unilateral* demonstrations of American power, like setting a precedent of responding militarily to such an escalation. The United States could, having sorted out in advance the choices to be made, elect to push for the unconditional surrender of a regime that had devastated a city. By statements of policy and principle to this effect, it could let the world know that it would be ready to launch preemptive strikes and to engage in preventive war if any such an attack seemed imminent again in the future.

Any very vicious use of nuclear weapons would seem to require a major intervention by the United States, to protect America's friends and interests, to terminate the nuclear exchange before the deaths climbed into the millions, and to punish the perpetrator so as to establish that this particular kind of nuclear escalation is *not* to be tolerated or repeated in the future. Such a vehement American reaction would apply particularly if the state was known to have only a very rudimentary nuclear arsenal. The initial use of nuclear weapons, even though not accidental, might in part have occurred because the state was so new to the possession of nuclear weapons and had not mastered the lessons learned over the decades by the existing nuclear weapons states. Such a state, hurrying to acquire nuclear warheads and then hurrying to use them, could hardly be trusted to revert to more restrained behavior after this first round of nuclear warfare.

Because such a perpetrator could not be very much trusted, and because it had less to hit back with in a second or third strike, the United States might well feel that an application of significant force could achieve an *unconditional surrender* of the regime involved, or at least its total nuclear disarmament.

This kind of policy response would be especially relevant if the perpetrator of the nuclear attack seemed as irresponsible and as undeterrable as the terrorists who launched the September 11 attack. The deterrent interaction of "mutual assured destruction" that has been successful between the great powers could not be relied upon to work in such a confrontation, and a continued possession of WMD by such actors could not be tolerated. In U.S. society, it is not legal for a proven killer to possess firearms.

This brings us back to the question of whether every launcher of nuclear attack in the next century will be a state or will have to have some state support. Our worst fear may indeed be that of nuclear terrorism, organizations like Al Qaeda stealing nuclear weapons or hiring renegade weapons designers from Russia or Pakistan to help them build their own. Some terrorist attacks require and presuppose a modicum of state support, while others can be carried off without the backing of any state.[36]

If we have strong reason to believe that a state regime is knowingly hosting or otherwise sponsoring the nuclear terrorist attacker, we have a motivational lever that we would not have otherwise. The sponsoring regime will care about retaining power, yet its collusion with the attackers, like the Taliban regime's support of Osama bin Laden and Al Qaeda, makes it an appropriate retaliatory target. The response to a nuclear terrorist attack, when it has a regime's backing, will be, as in the response to the September 11th attack, to punish that supporting regime by deposing it, thereby offering a deterrent lesson to other governments around the world, that they will face a similar unwelcome punishment if they enable a less responsible actor to launch a nuclear attack.

The caution remains that in the future not every terrorist nuclear attack will require state support. Where no state support was involved, the punishment would be more difficult to design, and deterrence would be much more difficult to achieve.

More generally, common sense dictates that the most pressing goal for American policy, after nuclear weapons had been used aggressively by a non-state, would be to terminate the destructive use of such weapons as soon as possible and, most importantly, to erase the impression that the introduction of such weapons had turned out to be profitable.

Some analysts might then ask what big difference nuclear weapons had made, for this response is quite parallel to the expected American response to the outbreak of *conventional* war, that is, terminate the conflict, punish aggression, and erase any impression that boundaries can be changed by military action. In this, the common sense of Americans reflects genuinely humane considerations about the outside world as well as the pursuit of America's own national interests.

The big difference, of course, stems from the enormity of the destruction that nuclear weapons can inflict, which will produce much more shock and horror than an outbreak of a conventional war and which might, under some circumstances, frighten *some* Americans into feeling that the United States should withdraw. In the net, the odds are that this will *not* be the reaction of most Americans, and that this will not be the policy which serves the total of American national interest. More probably, the unique destructiveness of nuclear weapons will make Americans feel a great urgency to intervene.

One scenario may seem wishful thinking by those who oppose all use of nuclear weapons, namely, that the introduction of nuclear weapons would turn out to be quite ineffective militarily and politically, as the forces attacked were not disabled, the country attacked not intimidated. What would the world's impression of nuclear weapons have been if the Japanese had simply continued fighting after the destruction of Hiroshima and Nagasaki, no more intimidated by those attacks than by the earlier conventional bombings of Tokyo and other Japanese cities. If the United States had then settled for a compromise peace in 1946 or 1947, allowing the Japanese to escape the occupation of their home islands, would not the entire world have rated nuclear weapons much lower as a deterrent and as a tool of intimidation? Would there not have been less impetus for nuclear proliferation since then?[37] One of the cases noted earlier was where a nuclear weapon is used to *again* bring an ongoing and horrible conventional war to a sudden close, and the world might applaud and heave a sigh of relief at this breaching of the nuclear taboo. But a very different result might emerge in the future, wherein such a use of nuclear weapons was *not* effective; whoever would have won the war without nuclear intervention still achieved victory, despite an opposing use of such weapons.

The latter scenario is most possible where the initiator of nuclear combat is a nuclear novice, rushing to use a very primitive atomic bomb, perhaps with an explosive yield far less than that of the Nagasaki bomb. But, more probable are the cases where substantial military impact is achieved by the use of a nuclear weapon, and/or horrible damage is inflicted on a civilian target.

The world would have less fear about subsequent uses of nuclear weapons if the only use after 1945 turned out to be laughably ineffective. But it would be wishfully self-deluding to *count on* such being the case, just as it would be delusional to conclude that nothing was accomplished when the Japanese cities were destroyed.

As noted above, there may also be cases where U.S. leaders do *not* feel it urgent to restore the nuclear taboo, or to "erase the gains" of a use of nuclear weapons, most especially where the gains of such a use were the repulsing of a conventional aggression, and where the gainer in using such weapons was a friend or ally of the United States. The difficulty with accepting any "good" use of nuclear weapons, however, is that it may set a precedent for a host of "bad" uses.

The qualitative distinction between conventional and nuclear weapons has been an important reference point for limited war and tacit bargaining restraints ever since the end of World War II, and most especially since the Soviets acquired their nuclear weapons in 1949. As Thomas Schelling noted four decades ago, such a distinction is difficult to resurrect once it has been muddied.[38] It has been much easier for all sides to stick to a policy of no use of such weapons than it would be to adhere to some newly drawn distinction of "some use under some circumstances."

Obviously, capabilities for mass destruction are growing, and they are likely to continue to grow. The North Korea that could threaten the city of Seoul with conventional punishment in 1998 might be able to threaten Japan and Alaska with nuclear destruction a decade later, and to threaten all the United States with such destruction a decade after that.[39] A continued effort to discourage the proliferation of nuclear weapons—as well as chemical and biological weapons—and of longer-range missile delivery systems is thus surely in order; and this is true now, before violation of the nuclear taboo, just as it would be all the more true after a nuclear weapon was used.

However, one can extract only a few strands of optimism from the past patterns of such proliferation. China in the 1960s looked like a rogue state in the bizarre style of its domestic politics during the Great Cultural Revolution and in the contempt it expressed for the international system of the outside world, but it mellowed on both dimensions in the three decades after it acquired nuclear weapons. Yet few would contend that one can count on such a change of attitude in North Korea, or even in Iran or Pakistan, that some kind of inevitable maturity would settle in with the possession of weapons of mass destruction.

While the reliability of possessors of nuclear weapons is not certain to grow, the degree of destruction the weapons can inflict is more likely to grow, as missiles increase in range and as other means of delivering warheads to targets emerge.

If nothing else, this suggests that some of the categories of response to a use of such weapons outlined here may be highly transitory. What would be the appropriate response to a nation that used nuclear weapons very soon after it had acquired them (when the residual portion of its nuclear arsenal would have to be small) might not seem so appropriate to the world if the same power behaved just as irresponsibly decades later, after its residual retaliatory capabilities might have grown much larger. And intervening in a nuclear war (to end it) between two fledgling nuclear powers will be much more difficult when both of them are no longer so "fledgling."

Nuclear weapons are still uniquely destructive. This uniqueness will make the United States government try to terminate any destructive use of them as rapidly as possible, while at the same time establishing the precedent that such escalation brings penalties for the perpetrator. Yet, because the United States will typically have preexisting commitments in any region where nuclear escalation occurs, abstract principle will have to be adapted. With regard to the alliances that the United States has developed since 1945, the policy guideline *for most cases* of nuclear escalation will have to be a massive effort to maintain and restore such alliances, to renew the confidence of America's partners, so that they can count on the same commitments as before the attack. In the absence of enduring commitment, such partners might race to surrender to the aggressors or to acquire their own nuclear weapons, feeling that the American deterrent could no longer be counted upon.

Even if the user of a nuclear warhead is a hostile state, a more obnoxious member of the international community, it might be very important for the United States to restrain any excessive retaliation by the victim of the attack, since the United States will have nuclear and conventional weapons options that other nations do not have, options for applying more tailored and measured punishments, and as it would be to the American interest, and to the world's interest, to avoid any open-ended escalation, which might devastate the entire world.

Ever since the end of the Cold War, the United States has thus found itself, deliberately or inadvertently, getting out in front of the world as a sort of "sheriff" for the maintenance of peace and collective security. Where the issues are whether and how to maintain the post-1945 restraints on nuclear weapons use, the United States has a related role to play. An example would be the efforts of the first Bush administration, in 1991, to keep Israel from becoming a major player in responding to Saddam Hussein's invasion of Kuwait, precisely because the response to the Iraqi aggression would be much more effective if it were led by the United States *without* the participation of a state that Iraq and the entire Arab world had long designated as an enemy.[40]

Two-Sided Nuclear Wars (Category F)

The following suggestion for what would be appropriate American policy if two countries were firing nuclear weapons at each other might seem particularly surprising, and unpleasantly counterintuitive. In the event of such a war, the United States might have to employ its own weapons, conventional and even nuclear, to intervene in the conflict, simply because the daily totals of people being killed and wounded would be so unacceptably high. And, rather than intervening on the basis of past alliances or going after a guilty party, the United States might have to join in disarming the *weaker* of the two opponents, on the simple logic that the exchange of nuclear rounds would not end until one of the arsenals had been reduced to zero. Determining which was the more guilty party would have to be reserved for later, with the bill and penalties being assigned then. But for the short run, the only consideration would be how to stop the nuclear attacks most quickly.

Some Americans might regard it as urgent that the United States intervene in *any* case where a nuclear weapon has been used to destroy a city. The sheer horror of such an attack would at the minimum dictate our supplying massive humanitarian aid to the survivors. More important still, however, would be deployment of American power, to prevent any immediate repetitions of such assaults and to punish the perpetrator, to deter further attacks.

One must stipulate that *some* of such situations would seem less urgently in need of intervention than others. If a single nuclear weapon had been expended to destroy a city, followed by a pause in such activity (perhaps because the victim had no such weapons to retaliate with), the affront to the world would be huge, but days and weeks might pass without any response from the outside world being necessary, while the exact conditions being imposed by the attacker were being hammered out.

Much more speedy action might be required, however, if the *victim* had nuclear weapons to hit back with, for there might follow round upon round of nuclear attack and counterattack. Similarly, more speedy action would be required if one of the sides seemed to be falling apart as a nation, creating the risks that its nuclear arsenal would get out of the government's control.

It might seem sad and morally unsound to have the United States joining in the preemptive disarmament of the weaker of any two adversaries that have gotten into a war, but this kind of "bandwagoning," by which the United States would join with the greater nuclear power to establish it as a nuclear monopoly within the region, might make the difference between tens of thousands of deaths and tens of millions.

If only one side to the conflict had nuclear weapons, it would be obvious where the first use came from. While this would make the nuclear attack seem all the more unfair and outrageous, the urgency of outside intervention would correspondingly be less.

If both sides possessed nuclear weapons, it would be more difficult to tell who was the nuclear first user. Each side might be accusing the other of being the violator of the taboo, or Side A might explain that its nuclear strike was intended to preempt a similar strike by Side B. For purposes of deterring such nuclear attacks in the future, it may be important to identify, and ultimately to punish, the *actual* first transgressor; but establishing the facts, as in analogous cases of the first side to launch a *conventional* war, would in many cases be difficult. If nuclear escalation emerged from a contest of nuclear-escalation "chicken," where each side is threatening such escalation during a conventional war, as during the Indian-Pakistani fighting in Kargil, the blame for the escalation would probably not be so obvious.

If, in a clearer case, the larger nuclear power had been the original aggressor, the moral tension might then be all the greater, because in the immediate term the United States might *still* have to side with the larger force, to disarm the smaller force before more of a nuclear holocaust was perpetrated. Then the *medium-term* American policy would have to be to try to impose requirements for reparations, and perhaps also nuclear disarmament, on the larger regional nuclear power. The means to obtain short-term halting of the nuclear war would violate the rules necessary for the long-term maintenance of law and order. But millions of lives might hang in the balance.

The case would be much simpler, of course, if the first user of nuclear weapons had been the state with the smaller nuclear arsenal. Punishing the nuclear transgressor would then be in perfect harmony with terminating the exchange of nuclear attacks and with keeping the nuclear weapons of this smaller power from slipping into totally irresponsible hands.

We must also address whether it would be appropriate to announce in advance the policy suggested here, that a democratic major power like the United States, in a nuclear war between two nuclear powers (like India and Pakistan, but we may see other such dyads in the future), would not always intervene on the side of an ally or of the victim, but would do whatever was necessary to terminate the nuclear exchange.

Such a policy clearly poses the moral hazard that it does not initially punish aggression nor reward restraint and that it does not honor and reward longstanding partnerships with the United States. To announce it in advance might thus be to send very much the wrong signal to powers around the world, and perhaps to undermine all parties that favor maintaining alliances and links with the United States. There may, realistically, have to be some very substantial differences between what the United States (and other democracies, and the outside world in general) *announces* as policy before a nuclear event, and what the *actual* policy would turn out to be in the event.

The most important broad general point being noted in this book is that a next use of a nuclear weapon (unless it fell into the "surprisingly benign" category) would come as an enormous and immeasurable shock to the world. The reactions to this shock might indeed shift the highest priority from maintenance of the nuclear taboo and nonproliferation to terminating the exchange, even at the cost of breaking the taboo, so that no more cities would be destroyed.

A modest and tentative proposal might be that the outside powers capable of intervening *not* announce the intervention strategy outlined above, but nonetheless contemplate it and prepare for it. It is possible that another new *declaratory* policy would emerge in the next few decades, an amendment to the grand posture of collective security, taking into account the uniquely destructive nature of nuclear weapons. Collective security prescribes that the *initiation* of warfare be punished, with outside-world interventions being guided by the elementary facts of who was the first to use arms. But the awesome nature of nuclear weapons may dictate that any *prolongation* of warfare be avoided, with the punishment for initiation being taken up a little later.

If the world, happily, never sees an outbreak of nuclear war, we may never see such an amendment to collective security proclaimed. If the world were to experience the horrors of a two-sided nuclear exchange, however, the aftermath might well include the proclamation of new intervention standards.

The argument here has been that the outbreak of a two-sided nuclear war, with massive casualties being suffered each day, would drive the United States and the other responsible powers to want to intervene urgently. But we should consider an alternative scenario in which the world witnessed a somewhat protracted two-sided nuclear war in the early rounds of which very few attacks had been on cities; but then a gradual escalation got under way, and the damage from the use of nuclear weapons grew as weeks went by. In such a scenario, at what point would the outside world be gripped by enough sense of urgency to find it time to intervene?

The Use of Established Nuclear Arsenals (Category G)

A somewhat different kind of policy stream emerges where the perpetrator of the first use of nuclear weapons since Nagasaki is a state with a much larger nuclear arsenal, a state like Russia, or perhaps soon enough China. Even if the indignation of the world and the United States were just as great as in the case of a nuclear escalation by Iran or North Korea, the options and choices would be substantially different. Totally eliminating the remaining nuclear arsenal of such a state would be a much more daunting, and perhaps impossible, task;

and the follow-up punishment that might be inflicted on the United States would be so massive as to put that option out of the question.

Here we would have to find a much more carefully managed array of tit-for-tat graduated punishments, while still holding most of the American retaliatory capability in reserve. (Were the escalator a power like Iran or North Korea, whose residual nuclear capability was much less and track record of rationality and amenability to mutual deterrence less, the United States might instead push for something like total defeat, because the task would be manageable and because the perpetrator could be much less trustworthy.)

These limits on what sort of retaliatory action was possible *might* suggest that the United States renew negotiations for substantial reductions in *all* nuclear arsenals, as the only plausible way to contain the threat and erase the impression that nuclear weapons would now be regularly in use. The world's moral reactions to a nuclear escalation would prompt new efforts at arms control, new attempts to reduce the arsenals of the nuclear powers. Such world moral opinion is never a perfect guide to policy, and rarely a stable asset in support of any policy choice; but the American national interest would be to exploit such opinion as much as possible, to rein in the future use of nuclear weapons. At the minimum, there might be greater plausibility in moves toward reducing nuclear arsenals and in moves by nuclear powers to narrow their criteria for using such weapons.

But the goal of *total* nuclear disarmament, of "a world without nuclear weapons," would hardly be easier to reach after a use of such weapons, because all the problems of verification would remain and because the assumption that nuclear weapons had somehow lost all their importance would have been dramatically challenged—by the simple fact that *someone* had indeed used them.

The American response to an escalation by a major nuclear power might well have to include acquisition of additional nuclear weapons, especially smaller nuclear warheads, so as to be able to retaliate at any level of destructiveness.[41] Especially if the escalating power had found some clever and finite way of employing such weapons, the United States would want to maintain a sense of "escalation dominance," that is, the ability to match each level of attack even while holding back something as an as-yet-unused retaliation for any higher-level attack.

The threat of "an eye for an eye" is a necessary part of nuclear strategy, fairly well understood for all the years since Nagasaki. If a nuclear escalation were characterized by *how little* damage was inflicted, it might be necessary for the United States to sharpen its tools, applying "surgical strikes" in response. The ability to hit targets accurately, with conventional warheads and even with nuclear ones, offers not only the ability to limit the collateral damage in an American response but also higher kill probabilities. It may be even more important now to be able to strike effectively at the particular homes or families of the leaders who were responsible for the nuclear attack, rather than at entire cities, cities where the bulk of the inhabitants were presumably innocent of any part in the nuclear escalation decision.

The challenges of precise strikes are not new to strategic calculation. The United States faced similar moral and practical difficulties in deterring the Soviet leadership during the Cold War. To make sure that deterrence worked (it apparently *did* work, since Soviet nuclear weapons were never used, and since the supposed Soviet advantage in conventional forces was never rolled into Western Europe), it was important to be able to target something that Soviet leadership *really* cared about; and our own morality was similarly troubled by any policy that would have involved killing innocent citizens of the Soviet Union as the punishment if a nuclear or conventional invasion had been launched.[42]

The same holds true even more today, when the nuclear attack we fear might be launched by a non-state actor, driven by a radical world-view and disgruntled with how the world is progressing. And the same applies in contemplating the deterrence of the Chinese Communist leadership or the North Korean leadership.

Effective targeted response requires hard-target kill-probabilities of a high order and the ability to reduce the collateral damage connected thereto. As noted, this will involve a larger array of non-nuclear and nuclear capabilities.[43] In terms of serving the American national interest, the best response to a nuclear escalation by a hostile leader might be a conventional warhead guided very accurately to that leader's place of residence.

If the power introducing nuclear weapons into combat was a major established nuclear power, our shock and anger might not be any less than if it were a state that had just acquired such weapons, but the realities of American policy choices would have to be much more constrained, just as they were during the Cold War. The residual destructive capacity possessed by the Soviet Union dictated that an American response could not be "all-out" unless the

Soviet nuclear attack had already been all-out. We focused instead on the option of "limited war" in various forms, including even "limited nuclear war"; and our policy planning for the future would have to include reviewing all the options that were considered during the years of the Cold War.[44]

The need for a comprehensive arsenal thus becomes an important argument for the renewed development (and testing?) of a wider array of nuclear weapons, some with larger yields and some with much smaller. As one wishes to contain and deemphasize the future role of nuclear weapons, however, the argument is also strong for devising *non-nuclear* options with which to hit back at an adversary, options which would punish the escalation and take away any gains it had achieved, options which by their mere prospect might, as in the days of the Cold War, deter any use of nuclear weapons in the first place.[45]

Designing responses to any enemy's climbing of the nuclear ladder has always been a very speculative and tentative exercise, at times running into dead ends, especially in the days of the Cold War when the Soviet Union seemed to have so many more conventional options than the Western powers had. It is important to be neither too pessimistic nor too optimistic when tailoring responses to nuclear weapons (or of other WMD) that might be launched by a major power. Those who are enthusiastic about relying *entirely* on conventional responses to such an escalation, in hopes that the United States can thereby avoid using nuclear weapons itself, thus taking the high ground of emphasizing denuclearization, are most probably guilty of wishful thinking. Yet it cannot be denied that if a major power used nuclear weapons for the first time since Nagasaki, it would be a most impressive achievement to punish and rebuff that power entirely by conventional means, thereby very much reinforcing the world's current intuition that nuclear weapons are not some kind of "ultimate weapon."

For a host of reasons, the arguments against any use of *American* nuclear weapons remain strong. These include the awareness that the United States was the inventor and only prior user of nuclear weapons, and the current impression that the United States is seeking to be some kind of hegemon, imposing its will on the world. But they also include the desirability of making nuclear weapons (regardless of the actual military realities) *look* less useful and relevant, the desirability of making publics around the world scoff at any proposals they hear from their own military establishments that nuclear proliferation had somehow become desirable.

It is undeniable that one can envisage *some* contingencies in which American nuclear weapons use would be the only possible response to some hostile initiative. But, where such responses can be avoided, where other means can be applied, the gains will be great.

If an adversary were to use chemical or biological weapons against the United States or an American ally or if such an adversary were even to use a *nuclear* weapon, the question would arise whether, and why, the United States would use a nuclear weapon in response. There are two very different kinds of logic supporting a nuclear response, each of which might in the end, however, steer us more toward a conventional retaliation.

The first logic is that an American nuclear response would be more militarily effective, capable of eliminating enemy capabilities that could not be eliminated in any other way. Perhaps a high-altitude nuclear detonation designed to produce electromagnetic pulse (EMP) effects could cripple a fledgling missile force on the other side that could not be crippled in any other way. Perhaps an earth-penetrating nuclear warhead could burn up and totally destroy a cache of biological weapons that, destroyed by other means, would do great damage to anyone downwind.

Such arguments for an American nuclear response in fact become arguments for renewed research on nuclear weapons design, and for a resumption of nuclear testing, because new warheads could be developed to accomplish particular purposes with less unwanted collateral damage. But, at the end of the trail of most analyses, applications of "surgical" nuclear responses have typically been very few, most of such weapons still being too burdened by substantial collateral damage to civilian population and structures.

A very different logic commending a nuclear response is that being willing to plan and execute such an attack constitutes a very necessary deterrent, without which adversaries would feel all too free to introduce any weapon of mass destruction they might possess. The prospect of "mass destruction" would be seen as the necessary potential response to mass destruction, simply as a motivational lever to keep such weapons from being employed in the first place. Since the United States and the other democracies do not possess chemical and biological weapons of their own, the nuclear response is the only plausible response to their use.

The problem with this second logic is that ordinary Americans and citizens of other democracies would typically be inclined to blame only the leadership, not the population, of the adversary nation for any introduction of WMD. Responding with a WMD would punish the innocent to get even with the few who are guilty, and this practice has always posed moral problems. A solution of sorts, during World War II, was for the Allies to tell themselves that most Germans and most Japanese were enthusiastic backers of the aggressions their countries had launched and that they therefore deserved to suffer the collateral damage imposed on them in the conventional bombings of Hamburg, Dresden, and Tokyo, and then in the nuclear bombings of Hiroshima and Nagasaki. The imposition of collateral damage is almost never welcomed openly and officially; it is always explained as somehow "inadvertent." But it has often been quietly welcomed, as a compellent or deterrent.

If a nuclear or other WMD attack were now to be launched by North Korea, even if it were followed by mass "demonstrations" in the streets and stadiums of Pyongyang endorsing the attack, very few outsiders would direct their anger at the North Korean population, because they seem so totally imprisoned and isolated by the Communist leadership. (There might well be anger directed at the opposing population if it were an Arab state that had launched a biological or nuclear attack, if Americans then saw televised scenes of Arab crowds enthusiastically endorsing the attack, for that malevolent enthusiasm would seem more spontaneous, less orchestrated, and more believable.)

There are many other good reasons for the United States to seek a conventional alternative response, rather than a nuclear response. One is avoiding a stigma that the United States is uniquely prone to employing nuclear weapons. But an additional powerful argument is that many ordinary Americans would be unable to accept any logic by which a nuclear response somehow serves a right and good purpose.

For reasons of historical imagery, there would also be definite advantages, *if* a nuclear response to some adversary attack were indeed to be required, for the United States to enlist partners in this, perhaps even enlisting the nuclear warheads of France and/or Britain, together with the air force capabilities of other partners from the democratic world, so as to avoid the image that only the United States would have used nuclear weapons again, and so as to diffuse the anger of the portion of the world that would be identifying with the target of the American counterattack.

To repeat a point made earlier, the permanent members of the United Nations Security Council, and most of the other countries of the world, are likely to be much more resolute and united in condemnation and response if someone has actually used weapons of mass destruction and/or has actually launched a blatant aggression than if they are confronted with mere allegations of a possible proliferation of WMD. In the latter case, they have been very unsupportive of an aggressive response, by the United States or any other country.

CHAPTER SIX

Some Final Observations

A final group of nuclear escalation scenarios might comprise cases in which attributes of the scenarios already described are mixed together in contradictory ways, making more difficult the sorting of priorities for American policy. These cases may run the greatest risk of catching us by surprise.

What if nuclear weapons were employed by a state that no one had anticipated was a nuclear power? Burma and Burundi, when mentioned above, struck us as totally implausible, but the next several decades may see nuclear weapons in the hands of not just terrorists but states where their mere presence will startle the world.

What if nuclear weapons were used suddenly, with no warning at all, with no conventional war or political crisis to set the stage, without prior brandishment? Or, nuclear escalation might be launched by a democratic government friendly to the United States, defying our stereotypes of how domestic politics translates into international behavior. A nuclear exchange might be launched by the weaker side in a confrontation, in a war that seemed suicidal, just as the Japanese attack at Pearl Harbor surprised most people, when the long-term odds seemed so totally against Japan if there were to be a war.[1]

Double Standards

It is indeed a challenge to our normal intuitions and logic that the entire history of the nonproliferation effort has been one of double standards, as the superpowers applied major efforts to discouraging or preventing other states, even their allies, from acquiring nuclear weapons, while maintaining large nuclear arsenals themselves.

It is not likely that an actual use of nuclear weapons would reduce the necessity for such double standards. However unfair it may seem for the United States and Russia to retain nuclear weapons while Japan and Germany and other states are pressured to forgo them, almost all of the policies that the

United States would need to adopt after a nuclear escalation would continue this kind of discrimination.[2] The judgment that the use of nuclear weapons in anger would somehow show the "moral flaws" in this double standard will not translate into serious policy guidance. For most of the imaginable cases, the American response to nuclear escalation would *still* be to seek to discourage non-nuclear states from acquiring nuclear weapons, and to discourage Israel from openly announcing possession of such weapons.

With regard to states facing the risk of internal civil war, Pakistan being a prime example, the appropriate policy for the United States may have to be to press for a *deproliferation,* by a mixture of threats and bribes, much more urgently than was the case regarding the nuclear weapons left in Ukraine, Belarus, and Kazakhstan after the breakup of the Soviet Union, but with the same end-goal, that all the nuclear warheads be removed from this territory.

Depending on the mode of delivery used for the nuclear attack, the United States might increase the urgency of its investment in missile defense systems. If the first nuclear warhead to be used since Nagasaki were delivered by a bomber or by a submarine or tramp steamer, the policy picture would be complicated by the need to mount other lines of defense as well. The attacks of September 11th were instructive. We now know that destruction can be inflicted on the United States by many means *other* than nuclear weapons, by means that might not even be anticipated by American planners until the actual event, such that NMD systems could be too easily by-passed. But one can also note how the World Trade Center attack demonstrated the hatred for America felt by various adversaries, and how it demonstrated their willingness to inflict large numbers of casualties on the American population. The logical conclusion is that *every* kind of defense needs to be reinforced.[3]

With regard to *defensive* systems, the United States would not pursue a double standard in the aftermath of a use of nuclear weapons, because it would be willing, and perhaps eager, to bolster the defenses of other threatened states. The less damage an attacker was able to inflict in any subsequent attack, the easier the task of the United States would be in the aftermath. If some other country were attacked and could then be provided with better defensive mechanisms, it would be easier to restrain the victim from inflicting retribution, with its risks of open-ended escalation. If the United States were itself the victim of the attack, having good defenses would make it less necessary to seek very substantial retribution and easier to convey to the attacker the impression that further nuclear escalation would be fruitless. Yet one hesitates to bet very much on the effectiveness of missile defenses.

As noted earlier, the United States may additionally need to augment its own array of nuclear weapons, to be able to respond with many different levels of retaliation. Much more debatably, the United States may want to share some of this technology for making nuclear weapon yields smaller and for making delivery systems more accurate with other states (with allies, and perhaps even with non-allies), all as part of cutting down on unwanted escalation and unnecessary destruction.

The appropriateness of sharing nuclear technology would be far more in doubt than sharing of defenses or command-and-control systems. Yet, in considering such policy decisions, we must be constantly mindful of the shock to the system that any actual use of nuclear weapons would amount to, and this shock might be enough to make thinkable all kinds of policies that presently seem out of the question.

The Actual Likelihood of Nuclear Use

It is obviously difficult to estimate the actual likelihood that nuclear weapons will again be used. The three most plausible of the cases discussed above are an escalation between Pakistan and India, use of a nuclear weapon by a terrorist like Osama bin Laden, and unpredictable behavior by North Korea.

With regard to a South Asian confrontation, it is easy to find strategic analysts in both countries who (sounding totally in agreement with each other) argue that mutual deterrence will work to keep nuclear weapons from being used, even if the countries go to conventional war, just as mutual deterrence worked between Moscow and Washington during the Cold War.[4] But such analyses by Indians and Pakistanis usually do not so fully reassure an outside observer.

Because of all the difficulties in determining how to *deter* a terrorist organization, the *only* real hope for averting the second kind of horror is a more resolute effort to head off all terrorist acquisition of nuclear weapons, and a major investment in the intelligence penetration of terrorist organizations so that the plans for such an attack can be anticipated and preempted.

All the other scenarios have to be added in as we try to sort out how real the threat is of another nuclear weapons use. The bulk of the analysis here has not pertained to whether this risk is large or small but to the nature of the likely aftermath and the plausible policy ramifications of such an escalation. Several generalizations can be offered at this point.

Deterrence can indeed work between Pakistan and India, or between any two other countries that might face each other with nuclear arsenals in the future, just as it worked between the nuclear superpowers during the Cold War. However, in the midst of that Cold War period, we were never *certain* that nuclear deterrence would work, and there were constant risks that it might fail. Whenever a political or military crisis emerges, as it did at the end of 2001 after the terrorist attacks on the Indian Parliament buildings, the risk of nuclear escalation goes up, as the weapons on each side are put on a higher state of alert and neither side wants to defuse the crisis by being the first to make concessions. If we were simply to relax our concerns about the reliability of deterrence in South Asia, we might sooner or later be very badly surprised.

Conversely, to assume that deterrence *definitely* will fail sooner or later, that the nuclear taboo will inevitably be erased, would be much too pessimistic, and the assumption might become a self-confirming hypothesis. If the strategists and policy planners and nongovernmental commentators talk excessively much about the likelihood of nuclear escalation, a preemptive logic may too quickly settle in by which we had better be ready to use these weapons tomorrow, because "they" are going to use them on the day after tomorrow.

But the counter to this, the *self-negating* hypothesis, may then turn out to be very useful for all human purposes here. As we consider how disastrous a nuclear escalation would probably be and how complex and difficult handling it would be, we become better prepared to take the profit out of such an escalation. In facing how terrible a nuclear event could be, we become more able to deter such an act and more committed to taking the proper steps to prevent and deter the *acquisition* of nuclear weapons in the first place.

This is thus, in the end, an argument for *contingent* analysis, an analysis that holds constant, rather than increasing, our estimates of the likelihood of nuclear escalation, but which sharpens our understanding of what others would do *if* such an escalation occurred and expands our understanding of what the United States would need to do.

Our contingent analysis would thus predict for 2015 or 2025 what it would have predicted for 1955 or 1975 or 1995, that nuclear weapons *may* come into use but are not likely to.

The Analogy with Other Taboos

The fear, once a taboo has been violated, is that what was regarded as unthinkable will no longer be seen that way. Yet, it would be too pessimistic to conclude that *any* violation of the nuclear taboo would shatter it. If the United States and the other responsible nations of the world are resolute in imposing punishments for a use of nuclear weapons (punishments ranging in size from nuclear counterattack and unconditional toppling of regimes to limited war, "graduated deterrence," and tit-for-tat responses), then the lesson will remain in place that such escalation is not something to be considered as part of a nation's normal menu of foreign policy options.

The taboo on incest remains in place in virtually every society because the whole world still shuns anyone known to be engaged in incest. The use of chemical and biological warfare continues to be regarded as shocking, and as somehow unnatural, even after a number of violations of the treaties and understandings banning warfare with such agents.[5] Similarly, the Indian and Pakistani nuclear detonations of 1998 did not see voters in a host of other nations concluding that now it was right and natural for them to acquire such weapons as well.[6]

The "taboo" label indicates that such behavior will be punished, but it always reflects a little more, an additional common sense that something unnatural has occurred. There are penalties for cheating on one's income tax, and people do not boast that they have done so, but such cheating is not the object of a taboo, a mystified sense that something unthinkable has happened. Incest and cannibalism do have this stigma, and the use of nuclear weapons has some of this as well.

The taboo on the use of nuclear weapons has not always been an asset for the United States and the other democracies, and it may not always be an asset. But redefining this taboo, reshaping this factor to tailor it as an asset for American needs, would hardly be easy.

If the Nuclear Escalation Is Delayed

The working assumption of this entire exercise has been that a new use of nuclear weapons is not necessarily likely but that it is something Americans and others need to think about. What we have been anticipating in our discussion is not a use in the next year or so (although the Indian-Pakistani confrontation of December 2001, while this study was under way, certainly gave one pause), but instead something that might happen in the next decade or two.

It is interesting to speculate a little further ahead, about what the problems and opportunities would be if this awful event were delayed and postponed for longer than this, so that we got past the year 2025 without another use of nuclear weapons.

The longer the taboo (or "customary international law") is observed, the stronger it may become, by some very persuasive lines of logic. This is, all in all, a powerful argument for deterring the use of nuclear weapons for as long as we can; even if a breaking of the taboo is inevitable, wouldn't it be nice if *one hundred* years had gone by before it happened, that is, if we got all the way to the centenary of the attacks on Hiroshima and Nagasaki, in 2045, without such an attack? The positive power of delay is also the argument for defining some ambiguous cases (analogous to the Israeli attack on Osirak and the possible attack on Three Mile Island) as nonviolations of the taboo; more precisely, this would be letting the "common sense" of the world define ambiguous cases this way, because world public opinion, although affected by the actions of states, nonetheless has a substantial life of its own.

One must face the fact that as the decades pass more and more countries may have acquired nuclear weapons, that the nonproliferation regime and the associated nonproliferation taboo will prove imperfect. A strong and continued effort at nonproliferation will still remain in order, rather than any pessimistic resignation to letting such weapons spread; it is important to note that the current number of separate states possessing nuclear weapons is far *lower* than was predicted in the 1960s and 1970s.

Because the dual-use overlap of peaceful and military technology is still greater with chemical and biological weapons than in the nuclear field, more and more countries may acquire chemical and biological weapons, the other "weapons of mass destruction."[7] It must be remembered how easily an attack with such non-nuclear WMD could be used to provoke a nuclear response, perhaps even from the United States.

The introduction of a biological weapon by an adversary in coming decades might produce more horrifying and extensive damage than a nuclear attack. Yet, as noted, such a biological escalation might not be immediately evident, taking hours or days for the disease to become manifest and perhaps weeks for it to spread into an epidemic. If a nuclear response to an introduction of non-nuclear WMD were deemed appropriate, a source of ambiguity would arise as to *when* the provocation for such a response occurred, and possibly from where. By contrast, in most nuclear escalations, it would be immediately clear what had happened, and determining the origin would probably be easier.

A more optimistic technological trend, but a trend not nearly as inexorable as the spread of deadly *offensive* nuclear, chemical, and biological expertise, is that the next couple of decades may deliver results on much more effective antimissile defenses, as well as defenses against bombers and cruise missiles, and defenses against all the more mundane means that terrorists and others could utilize to bring a weapon of mass destruction into the United States. One result of the anthrax mailing that followed the September 11th attacks is indeed that the United States may invest in vaccines to protect all Americans against anthrax and against a much more deadly threat, smallpox. But the trail of biological warfare, and the defenses against it, does not end so quickly there, for new offensive threats will emerge in the future.

The observations here are hence two-sided. The longer we look ahead into the future, the more numerous may be the powers capable of nuclear aggression. Almost certainly, the number capable of *provoking* someone else's nuclear escalation by an outrageous use of chemical or biological warfare will rise. But the longer the pattern of non-use of nuclear weapons is maintained, the stronger the feeling will be, around the world, that this is something "unthinkable," something which is simply not done.

An Exception to Prove the Rule?

Maintaining a "perfect record" of non-use of nuclear weapons up to the one hundredth anniversary of the bombing of Nagasaki might strike many readers as precarious, because they assume that one or another of the many scenarios we have listed here will become real. Even if we maintained the perfect record by defining away some situations that are more marginal (the use of a "garbage bomb" for example), many readers would regard this goal as too optimistic. Such a manipulation of definitions will remind baseball fans of cases when a game remains a "no-hitter" when the official scorer rules a play an "error" rather than a "hit"; but, as noted several times above, more than the record books and fan satisfaction will be at issue. The world's expectations will decide whether some marginal case is remembered as another nuclear attack after

Nagasaki, and there is always the real risk that such expectations will become self-confirming.

In the case of an actual attack, the most urgent task might be to focus on preventing repetitions of the event, by turning it into a lesson that using nuclear weapons does not reap rewards, does not solve problems, but merely brings defeat down on the perpetrator. If the perfect record of non-use of these weapons is broken and we are seeking grounds for optimism, our best hope might be that a single use would reestablish the historical pattern that had discouraged such use theretofore.

Hiroshima and Nagasaki, the only actual uses of nuclear weapons in history, do not amount to a model of this lesson, for the United States surely feels that it gained by destroying these cities; Japan surrendered quickly thereafter, in a war which Japan had initiated, in a war which most Americans dreaded would last several more years. The American occupation of Japan was made effortless by the destruction of Hiroshima and Nagasaki, and the lesson of 1945 was that nuclear weapons use could pay dividends.

The important point for the future, however, is that, under some circumstances, the *next* use of such weapons may *not* pay any such dividends. Some of the scenarios we have outlined for nuclear weapons use are purposeful and rational by the standards of most of the world, while others are not. As a policy tack, arranging the follow-up to a use of nuclear weapons so that gains are not achieved, so that normal state purposes are not served, could develop a lesson very different from what emerged in 1945.

The American Role

One very powerful argument against the United States being the next user of nuclear weapons, even in response to an adversary's use of some other kind of weapon of mass destruction, is quite obvious, but it nonetheless bears repeating: the record would be continued by which the United States remained the *only* nation ever to have used such weapons in combat.

It has been fashionable on the campuses of American and other Western universities, especially since the Vietnam War, to suggest that Americans are uniquely violent, uniquely troublesome for the world, because of the nature of the capitalist economic system (and even the traditions of cowboy violence); this is presumably illustrated by the high rates of gun ownership and homicide in the United States as compared with any of the other Western democracies.

This argument gets a sympathetic hearing around the world, even though one can easily construct very well-documented arguments that the 1945 use of nuclear weapons shortened World War II and that other nations also destroyed cities in World War II by aerial bombardment, only using thousands of bombers carrying conventional "block-busters" because they did not have the option of a single bomber carrying a nuclear "city-buster." None of this history erases the simple fact that Americans are alone in having used nuclear weapons, and none of this will ever keep critics, foreign or domestic, of American society and policy from conjuring up an indictment of American culture based on this.

Some critics even suggest that Hiroshima and Nagasaki also illustrate a basic American racism, claiming that the atomic bomb would not have been used on the Germans, fellow Caucasians, but was used on the "yellow" Japanese.[8] If the United States is called upon to initiate the use of nuclear weapons again, the targeted adversary most likely would be non-European, at this point most probably North Korean or Arab. Were there to be any such American nuclear attack on an Arab target, no matter what the explanation or provocation, the likelihood is that the Arab world, and the entire non-European world, would never forget or forgive this. (The same would hold true should there be an Israeli nuclear strike against an Arab target.)

All of these speculations are concerned with myths as well as realities, since, in political affairs, myths can so easily become realities. If people believe, regardless of the foundation, that nuclear weapons are basically unusable, such weapons are less likely to be used. If people believe that Americans are uniquely prone to inflicting destruction on other peoples and could easily use nuclear weapons again, such an interpretation of history, regardless of the foundation, will make it much more difficult for the United States to muster support around the world. Conversely, if the next use of a nuclear weapon is by another power, perhaps even against the United States, the legend would be disproved that *only* Americans could ever be so brutal as to inflict such an attack.

The various scenarios for another use of nuclear weapons would influence and be influenced by what the American role in the world will be in the future. One can speculate about how each kind of nuclear escalation would increase or decrease American political influence. Many factors will determine the extent of American influence in the coming decades. The appeal of American culture and life style may grow or it may wane. American conventional military power may surge far ahead of that of potential adversaries and of traditional allies, or it may be eclipsed by new technological revolutions and by the adoption of "asymmetrical" opposing strategic approaches. The American economy may grow faster or less fast than that of China or of united Europe. For the purpose of our survey, the analysis of the U.S. role will have to be more limited, considering how a nuclear escalation anywhere would affect the American leadership role in the world, and then how the handling of such an escalation might *depend on* the extent of American preeminence.[9]

One can imagine a *few* scenarios in which a use of nuclear weapons would enhance the American role in the world, especially if the perpetrator of the attack were particularly inept, an easy target for effective retaliation, and American conventional military power was brought to bear to repulse the aggression and depose the regime that had violated the nuclear taboo. In what might be regarded as a perfect opportunity to "set an example," if American military power and political influence played the major role, it might reinforce the United States' role as "sheriff," while the rest of the world applauded. An analogy could be drawn with the aggression of Saddam Hussein against Kuwait in 1990, which was effectively repulsed by American military power and political leadership, very much reinforcing that political leadership.

The use of power sometimes enhances a state's power, especially when the rest of the world largely approves of the way power was used. Much gets written around the world about how France, China, Russia, and India have had reason to fear American power since 1991, as the United States threatens to become a hegemon,[10] but most of the world generally welcomed this American preeminence, bandwagoning behind American leadership, rather than leaning toward balance-of-power resistance to this leadership.[11]

Yet only a small fraction of the scenarios we can address are likely to reinforce American leadership in this manner. For a great number of the ways that we can envisage nuclear weapons coming into use, the net impact would likely be very destabilizing and upsetting for world politics in general and include the risk that American leadership would not be as trusted anymore and that American influence would shrink.

A reduction in U.S. stature would be more likely than not if it had been *American* nuclear weapons that were used. Even were some other nuclear arsenal to come into play, we might encounter many of the less desirable kinds of aftermath noted above: some nations might opt out of any alliances or collec-

tive security arrangements, for fear that their cities would be added to the nuclear target list; some of the world's publics might directly blame the United
States, for having invented nuclear weapons in the first place and for having
kept open the option of nuclear escalation all through the Cold War and beyond; the *American* public might want their government to back away from
any crisis involving someone else's use of nuclear weapons; the United States
Congress, and perhaps even the president, might decide on retreat, in fear of
the risk that American cities would otherwise be the next to be destroyed. If a
future United States government were to run away from the leadership role
when confronting a use of nuclear weapons, the global trust in American leadership would most certainly be reduced.

As noted, the extent of American leadership around the world over the next
four decades, that is, in the years up to 2045, will depend on many different
factors, on the ups and downs of economies and populations, on revolutions
or the lack of same in conventional military technology, and on how wisely
American foreign policy is managed from administration to administration.
But there is a bottom line: a nuclear escalation anywhere around the world is
more likely to reduce American political influence than to reinforce it.

The question of how important American preeminence and leadership
would be in the handling of a nuclear escalation crisis provides a strong opportunity for those arguing against any new isolationism or American retreat
from the world. Since the end of the Cold War, a small number of American
political analysts have called into question whether "isolation" is really so
foolish or inappropriate,[12] and the administration of President George W.
Bush came into office with slogans promoting reducing the American role of
"policeman" in the world, which it said might include letting the opposing
sides in the Arab-Israeli confrontation settle more of their dispute on their
own and being involved in fewer "peacekeeping" interventions around the
world.[13] This tone of the foreign policy of the George W. Bush administration
was, of course, substantially altered in the wake of the September 11th terrorist attacks; but the issue remained open, with debates in both the Republican
and Democratic parties on whether the United States has to be playing a
major leading role, and a major coordinating role, in the world.

But, for most of the scenarios for nuclear escalation we can list, the only
way the aftermath could be managed effectively for world interests, and for
American interests, would indeed be for the United States to play a major leadership role, employing its own conventional forces, brandishing or even per-

haps *using* its own nuclear forces, and coordinating the military and economic responses of the other major and more minor powers around the world.

Any attempt to predict several decades ahead is, of course, fraught with unknowns. If the world has made it to the year 2035 without use of another nuclear weapon, will American leadership have been crucial in this success? If such an escalation occurs in the ensuing decade, will the United States have helped nevertheless get us safely to 2045? American economic, cultural, and conventional military power may have been reduced by then, as some other country or countries surge forward. If some other benign hegemon has moved, deliberately or inadvertently, into the role that America has played since the end of the Cold War, how much of the leadership responsibilities, of the role of "sheriff," will have been lifted from American shoulders?

In the more immediate future, there may be *some* scenarios for nuclear escalation that would be handled well, for world or American interests, *without* the United States' playing a major role. But the bottom-line assessment is that these will be quite few compared to the cases where it would be most important that the United States be centrally involved.

Proliferation with Moderation?

The possibility that North Korea is acquiring atomic bombs very much enlivens our concern that such weapons will be used, if only because so many North Korean actions in the past have seemed somewhat irrational, at odds with what would seem to be the regime's own interests. Yet a strand of optimism would emerge if Pyongyang were, like Israel and other conventionally threatened regimes in the past, to employ nuclear weapons merely to reinsure its existence in face of neighbors who regard it as vastly overdue for a regime change. If nuclear weapons are acquired by North Korea merely as a deterrent and power enhancement, to prolong the communist regime, this might seem lamentable to many; but it would not relate to the subject area of this book, the actual *use* of such weapons.

By another, more pessimistic, line of reasoning, a greater concern about ongoing nuclear proliferation is not that the new arsenals of nuclear weapons will come into immediate use but that the possessors of such weapons would feel emboldened to launch conventional aggressions, counting on their nuclear arsenals to deter intervention by the United States or other outside powers.[14]

If this were all that were to happen, it would be bad enough, but would again be outside the scope of this book.

Yet the negative flow of such proliferation is not so easily contained. Every crisis occurring under the shadow of opposing nuclear arsenals and every conventional aggression launched under the cover of a new nuclear force will pose some risk that escalation will occur and that nuclear weapons will indeed be used. The more proliferation, the more crises and the more risk of use.

Moreover, if a country like North Korea, by acquiring a capability for threatening North America with nuclear attack, were to scare the United States away from its role in protecting South Korea or Japan, Seoul and Tokyo could be counted upon to move into very new modes of conduct, ranging from acquiring their own nuclear arsenals to attempting to attack the North Korean force preemptively, all of which would significantly increase the likelihood that the nuclear taboo would be broken.[15]

Thus, while one can indeed imagine the next four decades with a *moderate* degree of nuclear proliferation and *no* nuclear use, every additional country that comes into the possession of nuclear weapons, whether a seemingly unstable and aggressive state or one that would act only in response, would pose the same concerns about whether they could settle into an enduring pattern of deterrence and non-use. Our concerns about this increased danger of nuclear weapons *use* thus form a powerful argument for greater efforts to prevent nuclear weapons proliferation.

Notes

ONE: Considering the Consequences of Nuclear Weapons Use

1. Useful data on the likely physical impact of nuclear explosions can be found in Samuel Glasstone and Philip J. Dolan, *The Effects of Nuclear Weapons* (Washington, D.C.: Department of Defense and Energy Research and Development Administration, 1977).

2. On the perceived likelihood of war after the Cold War, see Donald J. Kagan, Eliot Cohen, Charles Doran, and Michael Mandelbaum, "Is Major War Obsolete?" *Survival* 41, no. 2 (Summer 1999): 139–152; William Arkin, Damien Durrant, and Hans Kristenson, "Nuclear Weapons Headed for the Trash," *Bulletin of the Atomic Scientists* 47, no. 10 (December 1991): 14–19; John Ikenberry, *After Victory* (Princeton, N.J.: Princeton University Press, 2001); Christopher Layne, "From Preponderance to Offshore Balance," *International Security* 22, no. 1 (Summer 1991): 86–124; and Robert Jervis, "The Future of World Politics: Will It Resemble the Past?" *International Security* 16, no. 3 (Winter 1991–1992): 39–73. Considerably more pessimistic views are presented in Peter Lavoy, Scott Sagan, and James Wirtz, *Planning the Unthinkable* (Ithaca, N.Y.: Cornell University Press, 2000).

3. The possibly benevolent impact of economic interdependence in reinforcing peace is discussed in Dale C. Copeland, "Economic Interdependence and War," *International Security* 20, no. 4 (Spring 1990): 86–124.

4. For examples of analyses suggesting a greatly reduced significance for all military capabilities, see John Mueller, *Retreat from Doomsday: The Obsolescence of Modern War* (New York: Basic Books, 1989); and Eugene Gholz, Daryl G. Press, and Harvey Sapolsky, "Come Home, America," *International Security* 21, no. 4 (Spring 1997): 5–48.

5. On the potential endurance of the model of collective security demonstrated in response to Iraqi aggression in 1991, see Richard K. Betts, "Systems for Peace or Causes of War?: Collective Security, Arms Control and the New Europe," *International Security* 17, no. 1 (Summer 1992): 5–43; and John Mearsheimer, "The False Promise of International Institutions," *International Security* 19, no. 3 (Winter 1994–1995): 5–49.

6. For some reflective analyses of the real challenges in the post–Cold War world see Fred C. Ikle, "The Second Coming of the Nuclear Age," *Foreign Affairs* 75, no. 1 (January 1996): 119–128; and Robert Jervis, "International Primacy: Is the Game Worth the Candle?" *International Security* 17, no. 4 (Spring 1993): 52–67.

7. On Indian and Pakistani thinking about real uses of nuclear weapons, see Ashok Kapur, *India's Nuclear Option* (New York: Praeger, 1976); and Ashok Kapur, *Pakistan's Nuclear Development* (New York: Croom Helm, 1987).

8. The significance and impact of the September 11th attacks are outlined in "Reinventing War," *Foreign Policy*, no. 127 (November–December 2001): 30–47; and Bruno

Tertrais, ed., *Nuclear Issues in the Post–September 11 Era* (in English) (Paris: Fondation pour la Recherche Strategique, 2003).

9. The possible nuclear role in deterring Iraq from resorting to chemical or biological attacks is noted in Rick Atkinson, *Crusade: The Untold Story of the Persian Gulf War* (Boston: Houghton Mifflin, 1993), p. 86.

10. The complications for the other members of the "axis of evil" are addressed in Joseph Cirincione, "Can Preventive War Cure Proliferation?" *Foreign Policy*, no. 137 (July–August 2003): 66–69.

11. This kind of optimism about the impact of nuclear proliferation in general is outlined very well by Kenneth Waltz, *The Spread of Nuclear Weapons: More May Be Better*, Adelphi Paper No. 171 (London: IISS, 1981).

12. A useful overview of North Korean behavior can be found in Michael Mazarr, *North Korea and the Bomb* (New York: Macmillan, 1995).

13. Japanese considerations in future nuclear choices are discussed in Shawn Burnie and Aileen Mioko Smith, "Japan's Nuclear Twilight Zone," *Bulletin of the Atomic Scientists* 57, no. 3 (May–June 2001): 58–62.

14. The risks that Israeli nuclear weapons will be used are discussed in Yair Evron, *Israel's Nuclear Dilemma* (New York: Routledge, 1994).

15. For a reference to such Iranian statements, see George Perkovich, *Dealing with Iran's Nuclear Challenge* (Washington, D.C.: Carnegie Endowment for International Peace, 2003).

16. On the history of the American declaratory policy here, see Ivo Daalder, *The Nature and Practice of Flexible Response* (New York: Columbia University Press, 1991).

17. On crisis diplomacy and the Taiwan dispute, see Robert S. Ross, "The 1995–1996 Taiwan Strait Confrontation: Coercion, Credibility and the Use of Force," *International Security* 25 no. 2 (Fall 2000): 87–123.

18. The historical evolution of Chinese statements about the use of nuclear weapons is outlined in Avery Goldstein, *Deterrence and Security in the 21st Century* (Stanford, Calif.: Stanford University Press, 2000).

19. Some of such hints of a change in Chinese policy are noted in Alastair Iain Johnston, "China's New 'Old Thinking': The Concept of Limited Deterrence," *International Security* 20, no. 3 (Winter 1995–1996): 5–42.

20. See Joseph Cirincione et al., *Deadly Arsenals: Tracking Weapons of Mass Destruction* (Washington, D.C.: Carnegie Endowment for International Peace, 2000) for a useful projection of trends in weapons proliferation.

21. On this basic distinction in targeting, see Glenn Snyder, *Deterrence and Defense* (Princeton, N.J.: Princeton University Press, 1961).

22. On the impact of the presence or absence of live television coverage of human suffering, see Lee Edwards, *Media Politik: How the Mass Media Have Transformed the World* (Washington, D.C.: Catholic University of America Press, 2001).

23. On nuclear responses to attacks by other kinds of weapons of mass destruction, see Barry R. Posen, "U.S. Security Policy in a Nuclear Armed World," in Victor Utgoff, ed., *The Coming Crisis: Nuclear Proliferation, U.S. Interests, and World Order* (Cambridge: MIT Press, 2000): 157–190.

24. See Peter Gizewski, "From Winning Weapon to Destroyer of the World: The Nuclear Taboo in International Politics," *International Journal* 51 no. 3 (Summer 1996): 397–419; Richard Price and Nina Tannenwald, "Norms and Deterrence: The Nuclear

and Chemical Weapons Taboos," in Peter Katzenstein, ed., *The Culture of National Security: Norms and Identity in World Politics* (New York: Columbia University Press, 1996): 114–152; and T. V. Paul, "Nuclear Taboo and War," *Journal of Conflict Resolution* 39 no. 4 (December 1995): 696–717 on the evolution of the nuclear "taboo." On the broader development of the pattern of non-use of nuclear weapons, see Robert Jervis, *The Meaning of the Nuclear Revolution* (Ithaca, N.Y.: Cornell University Press, 1989).

25. On the evolution of a "customary international law" regarding use of nuclear weapons, see Nicholas Rostow, "The World Health Organization, the International Court of Justice, and Nuclear Weapons," *Yale Journal of International Law* 20, no. 1 (Winter 1995): 151–185; and Saul Mendlovitz and Peter Weiss, "Judging the Legitimacy of Nuclear Weapons," *Arms Control Today* 26, no. 1 (February 1996): 10–14.

26. On the slow emergence of the nuclear taboo, see Thomas C. Schelling, "The Legacy of Hiroshima: A Half-Century without Nuclear War," *Philosophy and Public Policy* 20, nos. 2–3 (Summer 2000): 7–13.

27. On the perceived taboos on these kinds of warfare, see Edward Spiers, *Chemical Warfare* (Champaign-Urbana: University of Illinois Press, 1986).

28. The nature of what became a "nuclear nonproliferation regime" is discussed in Harald Muller, "The Internationalization of Principles, Norms and Rules of Governments," in Volker Rittberger, ed., *Regime Theory and International Relations* (Oxford: Clarendon Press, 1995): 361–390.

29. On the variety of explanations for terrorists' abstention from using chemical or biological weapons, see José Vegar, "Terrorism's New Breed," *Bulletin of the Atomic Scientists* 54, no. 2 (March–April 1998): 50–55.

30. On the anthrax attack and the reactions thereto, see Christopher F. Chyba, "Toward Ecological Security," *Foreign Affairs* 81, no. 3 (May–June 2002): 122–137.

31. The Tokyo poison gas attack is discussed in Ron Purver, *Chemical and Biological Terrorism: The Threat According to Open Literature* (Ottawa: Canadian Security Intelligence Service, 1995); and Milton Leitenberg, "The Experience of the Japanese Aum Shinrikyo Cult and Biological Agents," in Brad Roberts, ed., *Hype or Reality: The New Terrorism and Mass Casualty Attacks* (Alexandria, Va.: Chemical and Biological Arms Control Institute, 2000), chap. 9.

32. The World War II abstention from chemical warfare is analyzed in Jeffrey Legro, *Cooperation Under Fire* (Ithaca, N.Y.: Cornell University Press, 1995).

33. On the Japanese experiments here, see Stockholm International Peace Research Institute, *The Problem of Chemical and Biological Warfare* (New York: Humanities Press, 1971), vol. 1, pp. 147–152.

34. The likely state of the Indian and Pakistani arsenals is outlined in George Perkovich, *India's Nuclear Bomb* (Berkeley: University of California Press, 1999).

35. On the Cuban missile crisis, see James Blight, *The Shattered Crystal Ball* (Lanham, Md.: Rowman and Littlefield, 1990); and Richard New Lebow, "Provocative Deterrence: A New Look at the Cuban Missile Crisis," *Arms Control Today* 18, no. 6 (July–August 1988): 15–16.

36. The nuclear shadow over the Yom Kippur War is discussed in Avner Cohen, *Israel and the Bomb* (New York: Columbia University Press, 1998).

37. See Anthony Preston, *Sea Combat Off the Falklands* (London: Willow Books, 1982), pp. 68–69 for rumors of British nuclear deployments through the war zone.

38. On the back and forth of the threats in 1991, see Atkinson, *Crusade*.

39. An important example of a simulation exercise about the future use of nuclear weapons, intended for research purposes more than for teaching, can be found in Marc Dean Millot, Roger Molander, and Peter Wilson, *"The Day After . . . " Study: Nuclear Proliferation in the Post–Cold War World* (Santa Monica, Calif.: RAND Corporation, 1993).

40. For some skeptical discussion of nuclear weapons tailored for the battlefield, see Stephen I. Schwartz, "The New-Nuke Chorus Tunes Up," *Bulletin of the Atomic Scientists* 57, no. 4 (July–August 2001): 30–35.

41. Some of such counterbunker scenarios for nuclear weapons use can be found in Stephen M. Younger, *Nuclear Weapons in the Twenty-First Century* (Los Alamos, N.M.: Los Alamos National Laboratory, 2000).

42. For such Iranian statements, see Perkovich, *Dealing with Iran's Nuclear Challenge.*

43. Some very pessimistic projections of the killing power of future biological weapons can be found in Jonathan Tucker, "Preventing the Misuse of Pathogens," *Arms Control Today* 33, no. 5 (June 2003): 3–10.

44. Some of the debate about grouping together "weapons of mass destruction" as a single category can be found outlined in Scott Sagan, "The Commitment Trap: Why the United States Should Not Use Nuclear Threats to Deter Biological and Chemical Weapons Attacks," *International Security* 24, no. 4 (Spring 2000): 85–115.

45. The relative success of the nuclear Non-Proliferation Treaty is discussed in T. V. Paul, *Power Versus Prudence* (Montreal: McGill-Queens University Press, 2000).

46. On the very different problems of overlap in peaceful and nonpeaceful uses of chemical and biological agents, see Susan Wright, *Biological Weapons and Disarmament* (Lanham, Md.: Rowman and Littlefield, 2003).

TWO: Some Scenarios of Nuclear Escalation

1. On the mysterious events of 1979, see Leonard Spector, *Going Nuclear* (Cambridge, Mass.: Ballinger, 1987), p. 222.

2. The "garbage bomb" option is noted in Richard Falkenrath, Robert Newman, and Bradley Thayer, *America's Achilles Heel* (Cambridge: MIT Press, 1998).

3. On the risks of attacks on nuclear power plants, see Bennett Ramberg, *Nuclear Power Plants as Weapons for the Enemy: An Unrecognized Military Peril* (Berkeley: University of California Press, 1984).

4. See Richard K. Betts, "Nuclear Proliferation After Osirak," *Arms Control Today* 11, no. 7 (September 1981): 1–3 for an analysis of the implications of the Osirak attack.

5. The evolution of South Asian nuclear capabilities is detailed in Bharat Karnad, *Nuclear Weapons and Indian Security* (New Delhi: Macmillan India, 2002); and Brahma Chellaney, "South Asia's Passage to Nuclear Power," *International Security* 16, no. 1 (Summer 1991): 43–72.

6. This possibility for the fourth September 11th attack is discussed in George Bunn and Fritz Steinhager, "Guarding Nuclear Reactors and Material from Terrorists and Thieves," *Arms Control Today* 31, no. 8 (October 2001): 8–12.

7. On the awesome possibilities of cyber warfare, see Thomas Homer-Dixon, "The Rise of Complex Terrorism," *Foreign Policy*, no. 121 (January–February 2002): 52–62.

8. On the possibilities of nuclear weapons with much lower yields, see William M. Arkin, "Those Lovable Little Bombs," *Bulletin of the Atomic Scientists* 49, no. 6 (July–August 1993): 22–27.

9. On use of "daisy-cutter" bombs in Desert Storm, see Rick Atkinson, *Crusade: The Untold Story of the Persian Gulf War* (Boston: Houghton Mifflin, 1993), p. 473.

10. On the basic nature of crisis diplomacy, see Richard Ned Lebow, *Between Peace and War* (Baltimore: Johns Hopkins University Press, 1981).

11. The Soviet 1962 thermonuclear tests are analyzed in Arnold Horelick and Myron Rush, *Strategic Power and Soviet Foreign Policy* (Chicago: University of Chicago Press, 1966).

12. For a discussion of this round of Indian and Pakistani testing, see Sumit Ganguly, "India's Pathway to Pokhran II," *International Security* 23, no. 4 (Spring 1999): 148–177.

13. For this Chinese episode, see John Lewis and Xue Litai, *China Builds the Bomb* (Stanford, Calif.: Stanford University Press, 1988), pp. 202–203.

14. The French sequence is outlined in Spector, *Going Nuclear*, pp. 25–32.

15. For an example of such critical skepticism, see Greg Mella, "That Old Designing Fever," *Bulletin of the Atomic Scientists* 56, no. 1 (January–February 2000): 51–57.

16. The tradeoffs in risk and cost between conventional and nuclear warfare here are discussed in Andrew Krepinevich and Steven M. Kosiak, "Smarter Bombers, Fewer Nukes," *Bulletin of the Atomic Scientists* 54, no. 6 (November–December 1998): 26–32; and John J. Midgley, *Deadly Illusion: Arms Policy for the Nuclear Battle* (Boulder, Colo.: Westview, 1986). See also the strong leaning toward conventional weapons demonstrated by game-players in Marc Dean Millot, Roger Molander, and Peter Wilson, *"The Day After . . . " Study: Nuclear Proliferation in the Post–Cold War World* (Santa Monica, Calif.: RAND Corporation, 1993).

17. Thomas C. Schelling, *The Strategy of Conflict* (Cambridge: Harvard University Press, 1960), chap. 8.

18. Such an interpretation of changed American national interest can be found in Jack Mendelsohn, "NATO's Nuclear Weapons: The Rationale for 'No First Use,' " *Arms Control Today* 29, no. 5 (July–August 1999): 3–8.

19. For a criticism of this continued reliance on the possibility of U.S. nuclear escalation, see George Bunn, "Expanding Nuclear Options: Is the U.S. Negating Its Non-Use Pledges?" *Arms Control Today* 26, no. 4 (May–June 1996): 7–10.

20. See Schelling, *Strategy of Conflict*.

21. On Chinese attitudes toward Taiwan, see Robert S. Ross, "Navigating the Taiwan Strait: Deterrence, Escalation Dominance, and U.S.-China Relations," *International Security* 27, no. 2 (Fall 2002): 48–85.

22. This implication of the September 11th attacks is discussed in Senator Carl Levin's, "A Debate Deferred: Missile Defense after the September 11 Attacks," *Arms Control Today* 31, no. 9 (November 2001): 3–5; and Dennis Gormley, "Enriched Expectations: 11 September's Lessons for Missile Defence," *Survival* 44, no. 2 (September 2002): 19–35.

23. A very early analysis of the risks of nuclear terrorism can be found in John McPhee, *The Curve of Binding Energy* (New York: Farrar, Straus and Giroux, 1974). For very recent analyses, see Graham Allison, *Nuclear Terrorism: The Ultimate Preventable Catastrophe* (New York: Times Books/Henry Holt, 2004); and Stephen D. Krasner, "The Day After," *Foreign Policy*, no. 146 (January–February 2005): 68–71.

24. On the comparative motivations for a counterforce or countervalue attack, see Charles Glaser, "Nuclear Policy Without an Adversary," *International Security* 16, no. 4 (Spring 1992): 34–78.

25. On the earlier logic of preserving the adversary's capital city, see William C. Martel and Paul L. Savage, *Strategic Nuclear War: What the Super Powers Target and Why* (Westport, Conn.: Greenwood Press, 1986).

26. The worrisome political instability inside Pakistan is outlined in Jessica Stern, "Pakistan's Jihad Culture," *Foreign Affairs* 29, no. 6 (November–December 2000): 115–126; and Anatol Lieven, "The Pressures on Pakistan," *Foreign Affairs* 81, no. 1 (January–February 2002): 106–119.

27. See Stephen M. Meyer, "How the Threat (and the Coup) Collapsed," *International Security* 16, no. 3 (Winter 1991–1992): 5–38.

28. The Cold War issues of nuclear command and control are discussed very extensively in Scott Sagan, *The Limits of Safety* (Princeton, N.J.: Princeton University Press, 1993).

29. For a discussion of the application of this logic to the Taliban in Afghanistan, see Milton Bearden, "Afghanistan, Graveyard of Empires," *Foreign Affairs* 80, no. 6 (November–December 2001): 17–30; and Michael O'Hanlon, "A Flawed Masterplan," *Foreign Affairs* 81, no. 3 (May–June 2002): 47–63.

30. For varying Cold War analyses of the relationship of psychology to nuclear deterrence, see Philip Green, *Deadly Logic* (Columbus: Ohio State University Press, 1968); Robert Jervis, Richard Ned Lebow, and Janice Gross Stein, eds., *The Psychology of Deterrence* (Baltimore: Johns Hopkins University Press, 1985); and Yehezkel Dror, *Crazy States* (Lexington, Mass.: D. C. Heath, 1971).

31. On worries about "loose nukes" in the former Soviet Union, see Jon Wolfsthal et al., *Nuclear Status Report* (Washington, D.C.: Carnegie Endowment for International Peace, 2001).

32. On the range of possibilities here, see Thomas C. Schelling, "Thinking About Nuclear Terrorism," *International Security* 6, no. 4 (Spring 1982): 61–77; and Jessica Stern, *The Ultimate Terrorists* (Cambridge: Harvard University Press, 1999).

33. The risk of nuclear weapons designers' becoming renegades is noted in William C. Potter, "Nuclear Exports from the Former Soviet Union: What's New, What's True?" *Arms Control Today* 23, no. 1 (January–February 1993): 3–10.

34. On Islamic and non-Islamic recourses to suicide attacks, see Ehud Sprinzak, "Rational Fanatics," *Foreign Policy*, no. 120 (September–October 2000): 66–73; and Jessica Stern, *Terror in the Name of God* (New York: ECCO, 2003).

35. Steven Kull and I. M. Destler are somewhat dismissive of worries about American or other resolve in face of such threats, in *Misreading the Public: The Myth of a New Isolationism* (Washington, D.C.: Brookings Institution Press, 1999). But the evidence from the RAND "Day After" simulations suggested that American leaders might want to stay out of a nuclear conflict except in the Middle East or Korea: Millot, Molander, and Wilson, *"The Day After . . . " Study*.

36. On the prospects of anti-missile defense protection for American allies, see M. Swaine, R. Swanger, and T. Kawaskami, *Japan and Ballistic Missile Defense* (Santa Monica, Calif.: RAND Corporation, 2001); and John Newhouse, "The Missile Defense Debate," *Foreign Affairs* 80, no. 4 (July–August 2001): 97–109.

37. The very delicate question of whether the United States would acquire missile defense protection for use not just against "rogue states" but against the other major nuclear powers is discussed in Dean Wilkening, *Ballistic-Missile Defense and Strategic Stability*, Adelphi Paper No. 334 (London: IISS, 2000); Charles Glaser and Steven Fetter,

"National Missile Defense and the Future of U.S. Nuclear Weapons Policy," *International Security* 26, no. 1 (Summer 2001): 40–92; and James Lindsay et al., *Defending America: The Case for Limited National Missile Defense* (Washington, D.C.: Brookings Institution Press, 2001).

38. Pierre Gallois, *The Balance of Terror* (Boston: Houghton-Mifflin, 1961).

39. Kenneth Waltz, *The Spread of Nuclear Weapons: More May Be Better*, Adelphi Paper No. 171 (London: IISS, 1981).

40. This kind of prediction about world reactions can be found in Elliot Abrams, *Close Call, Intervention, Terrorism, Missile Defense and "Just War"* (Washington, D.C.: Ethics and Public Policy Center, 1998).

41. Mao's very provocative statements here are noted in Leonard Beaton and John Mattox, *The Spread of Nuclear Weapons* (London: Institute for Strategic Studies, 1962), p. 132. See also Lewis and Xue, *China Builds the Bomb*, chap. 3.

42. For a discussion of whether the logic of "catalytic escalation" was ever very much involved in the French "force de frappe," see David S. Yost, "French Nuclear Targeting," in Desmond Ball and Jeffrey Richelson, eds., *Strategic Nuclear Targeting* (Ithaca, N.Y: Cornell University Press, 1986), p. 134.

43. Skepticism on whether new nuclear weapons states are bound to become mature in their use of such weapons is to be found in Lewis Dunn, *Containing Nuclear Proliferation*, Adelphi Paper No. 263 (London: IISS, 1991).

44. On the Communist regime in Pyongyang and its seeming idiosyncracies, see Leon Sigal, *Disarming Strangers* (Princeton, N.J.: Princeton University Press, 1998); and Selig Harrison, *Korean Endgame* (Princeton, N.J.: Princeton University Press, 2002).

45. Such a more coldly calculating rationale for North Korean nuclear weapons is discussed in Victor D. Cha and David C. Kang, "The Korean Crisis," *Foreign Policy*, no. 136 (May–June 2003): 20–29.

46. The "pariah state" concept was first presented by Robert Harkavy in "The Pariah State Syndrome," *Orbis* 21, no. 4 (Fall 1977): 623–649.

47. The back and forth of U.S. nuclear policies toward Korea is recounted in Robert Manning, "The United States and the Endgame in Korea," *Asian Survey* 37, no. 7 (January 1997): 597–608; and in Victor Cha, *Alignment Despite Antagonism: The United States–Korea–Japan Security Triangle* (Stanford, Calif.: Stanford University Press, 1999).

48. For such an expression of confidence in mutual deterrence, see K. Subrahmanyam, "Regional Conflicts and Nuclear Fears," in Herbert Levine and David Carlton, eds., *The Nuclear Arms Race Debated* (New York: McGraw-Hill, 1986). For an opposite interpretation, see Andrew C. Winner and Tosh Yoshihara, "India and Pakistan at the Edge," *Survival* 44, no. 3 (Autumn 2002): 69–86.

49. Some examples of Cold War analysis of "limited nuclear warfare" may be found in Desmond Ball, "The Development of the SIOP," in Desmond Ball and Jeffrey Richelson, eds., *Strategic Nuclear Targeting* (Ithaca, N.Y.: Cornell University Press, 1986), pp. 57–83.

THREE: Likely World Reactions

1. Details on the Osirak attack can be found in Shai Feldman, "The Attack on Osiraq—Revisited," *International Security* 7, no. 2 (Fall 1982): 114–142.

2. On the nuclear depth-charge issue in the Falklands War, see Anthony Preston, *Sea Combat Off the Falklands* (London: Willow Books, 1982), pp. 68–69.

3. A discussion measuring the impact of 9/11 on the American public and the world's public can be found in articles by Ashton Carter, Philip Heymann, Barry Posen, and Stephen Walt in "The Threat of Terrorism: U.S. Policy After September 11," *International Security* 26, no. 3 (Winter 2001–2002): 5–78.

4. On the techniques for bomb identification, see Paul Leventhal and Yonah Alexander, eds., *Preventing Nuclear Terrorism* (Lexington, Mass.: D. C. Heath, 1987).

5. On "loose nukes" in the former Soviet Union, see also William C. Potter, "Before the Deluge? Assessing the Threat of Nuclear Leakage from the Post-Soviet States," *Arms Control Today* 25, no. 8 (October 1995): 9–16.

6. On the general command-and-control issue here, see Peter D. Feaver "Command and Control in Emerging Nuclear Nations," *International Security* 17, no. 3 (Winter 1992–1993): 160–187.

7. On the 2003 disarray in the Western alliance, see Chris Patten, "Democracy Doesn't Flow from the Barrel of a Gun," *Foreign Policy*, no. 138 (September–October 2003): 40–45.

8. The results of the UN inspections are discussed in Frank Ronald Cleminson, "What Happened to Saddam's Weapons of Mass Destruction?" *Arms Control Today* 33, no. 7 (September 2003): 3–6.

9. On the tone of the George W. Bush administration, see John Lewis Gaddis, "Bush's Security Strategy," *Foreign Policy*, no. 133 (November–December 2002): 50–57; and Robert Kagan, "The World and President Bush," *Survival* 43, no. 1 (Spring 2001): 7–16.

10. An American criticism of the unilateral approach can be found in Jeffrey W. Legro and Andrew Moravcsik, "Faux Realism," *Foreign Policy*, no. 125 (July–August 2001): 80–82.

11. On the comparative decline in world resolve against Saddam Hussein, see James P. Rubin, "Stumbling into War," *Foreign Affairs* 82, no. 5 (September–October 2003): 46–66.

12. For a longer elaboration of this author's views on this contingency, see George H. Quester, "The Response to Renegade Use of Weapons of Mass Destruction," in Victor Utgoff, ed., *The Coming Crisis: Nuclear Proliferation, U.S. Interests and World Order* (Cambridge: MIT Press, 2000), pp. 227–244.

13. The impact of global news operations like CNN is discussed in Lee Edwards, *Media Politik: How the Mass Media Have Transformed the World* (Washington, D.C.: Catholic University of America Press, 2001).

14. For earlier analyses of the inherent problems in influencing an aggressor, see Herman Kahn, *On Escalation* (New York: Praeger, 1965).

15. The American feelings toward "limited war" are analyzed thoroughly in Robert E. Osgood, *Limited War: The Challenge to American Strategy* (Chicago: University of Chicago Press, 1957).

16. The vulnerability of existing alliance structures is analyzed in Jonathan Stevenson, "How Europe and America Defend Themselves," *Foreign Affairs* 82, no. 2 (March–April 2003): 75–90; and Douglas Eden, ed., *Europe and the Atlantic Relationship* (New York: St. Martin's Press, 2000).

17. The world's rallying behind the United States after September 11th is discussed in William Maley, *The Afghanistan Wars* (Basingstoke, England: Palgrave Macmillan, 2002).

18. On the historic need for a leading power to anticipate coalitions among weaker powers, see Hans Morgenthau, *Politics Among Nations* (New York: Knopf, 1967).

19. On "bandwagoning" versus "balancing," see Stephen M. Walt, *The Origins of Alliances* (Ithaca, N.Y.: Cornell University Press, 1987).

20. For some examples of "realist" analysis, see David Shambaugh, "China's Military Views the World," *International Security* 24, no. 3 (Winter 1999–2000): 52–79.

21. On the limits of American conventional military capabilities, see Stephen M. Walt, "Musclebound: The Limits of U.S. Power," *Bulletin of the Atomic Scientists* 55, no. 2 (March–April 1999): 44–48.

22. On the actual deadly experience in 1945, see Robert Trumbull, *Nine Who Survived Hiroshima and Nagasaki* (New York: Dutton, 1987).

23. For examples of reasoned calls for such total nuclear disarmament, see Stansfield Turner, *Caging the Nuclear Genie* (Boulder, Colo.: Westview, 1997); Jonathan Schell, *The Abolition* (New York: Knopf, 1984); Michael Mazarr, ed., *Nuclear Weapons in a Transformed World* (New York: St. Martin's Press, 1997); and Harold Feiveson, ed., *The Nuclear Turning Point* (Washington, D.C.; Brookings Institution Press, 1999).

24. On the inherent difficulties of total nuclear disarmament, see Kathleen Bailey, "Why We Have to Keep the Bomb," *Bulletin of the Atomic Scientists* 51, no. 1 (January–February 1996): 30–37; and Robert A. Manning, "The Nuclear Age: The Next Chapter," *Foreign Policy*, no. 109 (Winter 1997–1998): 70–84.

25. The risks of a "nuclear war that nobody wanted" at lower nuclear force levels are noted in Michael Quinlan, "British Nuclear Policy: Past, Present and Future," in John C. Hopkins and Weixing Hu, eds., *Strategic Views from the Second Tier* (San Diego: University of California Institute on Global Conflict and Cooperation, 1994): 125–140.

26. For a critique of proposals for an expanded and more finely tuned nuclear arsenal, see Sydney Drell, James Goodby, Raymond Jeanlez, and Robert Peurifoy, "A Strategic Choice: New Bunker Busters versus Nonproliferation," *Arms Control Today* 83, no. 2 (March 2003): 8–10.

27. On the countries that abandoned dreams of acquiring nuclear weapons, see Mitchell Reiss, *Without the Bomb* (New York: Columbia University Press, 1988).

28. On the difficulties of a reliable deproliferation, see Ariel E. Levite, "Never Say Never Again: Nuclear Reversal Revisited," *International Security* 27, no. 3 (Winter 2002–2003): 59–88.

29. For some of such South Asian arguments see Jasjit Singh, ed., *Nuclear India* (New Delhi: Knowledge World, 1998); and K. Subrahmanyam, ed., *Security in a Changing World* (Delhi: BR Publishing House, 1990). An important outsider's reflections on this can be found in Michael Quinlan, "How Robust Is India-Pakistan Deterrence?" *Survival* 42, no. 4 (Winter 2000–2001): 141–154.

30. For an analysis of the immediate American popular reaction to September 11th, see Stephen E. Flynn, "America the Vulnerable," *Foreign Affairs* 81, no. 1 (January–February 2002): 60–74.

31. For a discussion of this kind of Japanese posture with regard to the nuclear issue, and its impact on the world, see Thomas Berger, "From Sword to Chrysanthemum," *International Security* 17, no. 4 (Spring 1993): 119–150.

32. On Japanese handling of plutonium, see Andrew Hanami, *The Military Might of Modern Japan* (Dubuque, Iowa: Kendall/Hunt, 1998).

33. Japan's latent nuclear weapons capability is assessed in Selig Harrison, *Japan's Nuclear Posture* (Washington, D.C.: Carnegie Endowment for International Peace, 1996).

34. For an optimistic assessment of whether Japan will abstain from reaching for its own nuclear weapons, see M. Kamiya, "Nuclear Japan: Oxymoron or Coming Soon?" *Washington Quarterly* 26, no. 1 (Winter 2002–2003): 63–75.

FOUR: Likely American Popular Reactions

1. On the "ambiguous" or "opaque" nature of the Israeli nuclear program, see Benjamin Frankel, ed., *Opaque Nuclear Proliferation* (London: Frank Cass, 1991).

2. The lingering possibility that the United States would see a need to escalate to nuclear weapons use is discussed in David Gompert, Kenneth Watman, and Dean Wilkening, "Nuclear First Use Revisited," *Survival* 37, no. 3 (Autumn 1995): 7–26.

3. The Cold War issues of responsibility are discussed at some length in Bruce C. Blair, *Strategic Command and Control* (Washington, D.C.: Brookings Institution Press, 1985).

4. The possibilities of such anonymous use are among the problems analyzed in Paul Leventhal and Yonah Alexander, eds., *Nuclear Terrorism: Defining the Threat* (Washington, D.C.: Pergamon-Brasseys, 1986).

5. Earlier failures of the American people to demonstrate unity and resolve are detailed in Alexander DeConde, ed., *Isolation and Security* (Durham, N.C.: Duke University Press, 1957).

6. For an illustration of the tendency of foreign leaders to underestimate American resolve, see Janice Gross Stein, "Deterrence and Compellence in the Gulf, 1990–1991: A Failed or Impossible Task?" *International Security* 17, no. 2 (Fall 1992): 147–179.

7. Some of the pitfalls the democratic process creates for effective foreign policy are outlined in Robert E. Osgood, *Ideals and Self-Interest in American Foreign Relations* (Chicago: University of Chicago Press, 1953).

8. The explanations for the early-twentieth-century American turn toward isolationism are discussed in Selig Adler, *The Isolationist Impulse* (New York: Free Press, 1957).

9. On the more unilateral tone adopted during George W. Bush's first term, see Morton Abramowitz, "Dear Dubya," *Foreign Policy*, no. 130 (May–June 2002): 78–79.

10. Some arguments for lessened reliance on forward bases are discussed in Michael O'Hanlon, "Can High Technology Bring U.S. Troops Home?" *Foreign Policy*, no. 113 (Winter 1998–1999): 72–86; and Eugene Gholz, Daryl Press, and Harvey Sapolsky, "Come Home, America," *International Security* 21, no. 4 (Spring 1997): 5–48.

11. For a survey of the many other kinds of misery that might be inflicted on the world in coming decades, besides nuclear war, see Lloyd J. Dumas, *Lethal Arrogance: Human Fallibility and Dangerous Technologies* (New York: St. Martin's Press, 1999).

12. For discussions of the anthrax menace, see Ken Alibek, *Biohazard* (New York: Random House, 1999).

13. Janne Nolan, ed., *Global Engagement: Cooperation and Security in the 21st Century* (Washington, D.C.: Brookings Institution Press, 1994) presents a collection of arguments for extensive intervention around the world, but on a very multilateral basis.

14. On the basics of the logic of collective security, see Inis Claude, *Power and International Relations* (New York: Random House, 1962).

15. On this basic American aversion to limits in warfare, see Morton Halperin, *Limited War in the Nuclear Age* (New York: John Wiley, 1963).

16. Attitudes of Americans toward limited war during the Korean War are outlined in Rosemary Foot, *The Wrong War: American Policy and the Dimensions of the Korean Conflict, 1950–1953* (Ithaca, N.Y.: Cornell University Press, 1985).

17. On Truman's loss of popularity because of the restraints he was imposing on the American military effort, see John W. Spanier, *The Truman-MacArthur Controversy and the Korean War* (Cambridge, Mass.: Belknap Press, 1959).

18. The exploitation of the threat of escalation is outlined in Bernard Brodie, *Escalation and the Nuclear Option* (Princeton, N.J.: Princeton University Press, 1966).

19. For recent statements on the possibilities of nuclear escalation, see Wolfgang K. H. Panofsky and George Bunn, "The Doctrine of the Nuclear-Weapons States and the Future of Non-Proliferation," *Arms Control Today* 24, no. 6 (July–August 1994): 3–9.

20. On the general American willingness to intervene, see Richard Haas, *Intervention* (Washington, D.C.: Carnegie Endowment for International Peace, 1996).

21. The basic logic of "graduated deterrence" is outlined quite clearly in Glenn Snyder, *Deterrence and Defense* (Princeton, N.J.: Princeton University Press, 1961).

22. For an example of such a demand for moral consistency, see William Epstein, *The Last Chance* (New York: Free Press, 1976).

23. Such a case for American "escalation dominance" is presented in Ariel E. Levite and Elizabeth Sherwood-Randall, "The Case for Discriminate Force," *Survival* 44, no. 4 (Winter 2002–2003): 81–98.

24. For a review of the many measures that would need to be taken to have an effective homeland defense, see Michael E. O'Hanlon et al., *Protecting the American Homeland* (Washington, D.C.: Brookings Institution Press, 2002).

25. On the willingness to trade classic American liberties for security when the external threat looms so much larger, see Richard C. Leone and Greg Anrig, eds., *The War on Our Freedoms: Civil Liberties in an Age of Terrorism* (New York: Public Affairs Press, 2003).

26. On the "lessons" of Vietnam, see Guenther Lewy, *America in Vietnam* (New York: Oxford University Press, 1978).

FIVE: Appropriate United States Policy Responses

1. On the likely dominance of the United States into the foreseeable future, see Stephen G. Brooks and William C. Wohlfurth, "American Primacy in Perspective," *Foreign Affairs* 81, no. 4 (July–August 2002): 20–33.

2. For such a benign interpretation of American salience, see Joseph Joffe, "How America Does It," *Foreign Affairs* 76, no. 5 (September–October 1992): 13–27; and Robert Kagan, "The Benevolent Empire," *Foreign Policy*, no. 111 (Summer 1998): 24–35.

3. An overview of the alternative sides in the 2003 disputes about how to confront Saddam Hussein can be found in Mark Strauss, "Attacking Iraq," *Foreign Policy*, no. 129 (March–April 2002): 14–19; and John J. Mearsheimer and Stephen M. Walt, "Iraq: The Unnecessary War" *Foreign Policy*, no. 134 (January–February 2003): 50–59.

4. For analyses matching this interpretation, see Joshua Muravchik, *The Imperative of American Leadership* (Washington, D.C.: American Enterprise Institute, 1996).

5. For the possibilities that American sovereignty would be eroded by some new "customary international law," see Steven R. Ratner, "International Law: The Trials of Global Norms," *Foreign Policy*, no. 110 (Spring 1998): 65–81.

6. On the arguments against a stronger international law, see Henry Kissinger, "The Pitfalls of Universal Jurisdiction," *Foreign Affairs* 80, no. 4 (July–August 2001): 86–96.

7. On the implications of the United States' accepting the restrictions of "no first use," see Richard Ullmann, "No First Use of Nuclear Weapons," *Foreign Affairs* 50, no. 4 (July 1972): 669–683.

8. The difficulties of making extended nuclear deterrence credible are outlined in Herman Kahn, *On Escalation* (New York: Praeger, 1965).

9. A presentation of the issues in maintaining extended nuclear deterrence can be found in David S. Yost, *The U.S. and Nuclear Deterrence in Europe*, Adelphi Paper No. 326 (London: IISS, 1999).

10. On Khrushchev's use of massive H-bomb tests, see Arnold Horelick and Myron Rush, *Strategic Power and Soviet Foreign Policy* (Chicago: University of Chicago Press, 1966).

11. The motives for the Indian and Pakistani test detonations are discussed in Hilary Synnott, *The Causes and Consequences of South Asia's Nuclear Tests*, Adelphi Paper No. 332 (London: IISS, 1999).

12. Speculation about "demonstration shots" can be found in Kahn, *On Escalation*.

13. On the argument that the United States would now profit from eliminating the nuclear option, see Ivo Daalder, "Nuclear Weapons in Europe: Why Zero Is Better," *Arms Control Today* 23, no. 1 (January–February 1993): 15–18.

14. For a review of U.S. governmental leanings toward the continued need for extended nuclear deterrence, see Kurt Guthe, *The Nuclear Posture Review: How Is the "New Triad" New?* (Washington, D.C.: Center for Strategic and Budgetary Assessments, 2002).

15. The American decision to renounce the possession of these other weapons of mass destruction is chronicled in Jonathan B. Tucker, "A Farewell to Germs: The U.S. Renunciation of Biological and Toxin Warfare, 1969–1970," *International Security* 27, no. 1 (Summer 2002): 107–148.

16. On the difficulties of finding a perfect deterrent to an adversary's use of chemical or biological weapons, see David Gompert, Kenneth Watman, and Dean Wilkening, "Nuclear First Use Revisited," *Survival* 37, no. 3 (Autumn 1995): 7–26.

17. Supporting this argument would be Robert G. Joseph and John Reichart, "The Case for Nuclear Deterrence Today," *Orbis* 42, no. 1 (Winter 1998): 7–19; and Robert C. Spulak, "The Case in Favor of U.S. Nuclear Weapons," *Parameters* 27, no. 1 (Spring 1997): 106–118.

18. For arguments against the desirability of the "WMD" category, see Wolfgang K. H. Panofsky, "Dismantling the Concept of 'Weapons of Mass Destruction,'" *Arms Control Today* 28, no. 3 (April 1998): 3–8.

19. On the nuclear element in the South Atlantic war, see Anthony Preston, *Sea Combat Off the Falklands* (London: Willow Books, 1982), pp. 68–69.

20. On possible Israeli use of nuclear weapons if the Sinai War had gotten out of hand in conventional terms, see Yair Evron, *Israel's Nuclear Dilemma* (New York: Routledge, 1994).

21. On this point, see again Thomas C. Schelling, *The Strategy of Conflict* (Cambridge: Harvard University Press, 1960), chap. 3.

22. On the normal erosion of command and control as a war moves along, see Bruce C. Blair, *Strategic Command and Control* (Washington, D.C.: Brookings Institution Press, 1985).

23. Some of the issues on sharing nuclear command-and-control devices are outlined in Scott D. Sagan, "The Perils of Proliferation: Organization Theory, Deterrence Theory and the Spread of Nuclear Weapons," *International Security* 18, no. 4 (Spring 1994): 66–107; and Peter D. Feaver, "Command and Control in Emerging Nuclear Nations," *International Security* 17, no. 3 (Winter 1992–1993): 160–187.

24. On the dangers of any launch-on-warning arrangements, see Scott Sagan, *The Limits of Safety* (Princeton, N.J.: Princeton University Press, 1993).

25. For a discussion of screening processes for handlers of nuclear weapons, which have become standard in the United States, see Herbert L. Adams, "Human Reliability, Instability, and the Control of Nuclear Weapons," in Hakan Wiberg et al., eds., *Inadvertent Nuclear War* (New York: Pergamon, 1993), chap. 6; and Paul Bracken, *The Command and Control of Nuclear Weapons* (New Haven, Conn.: Yale University Press, 1983).

26. This complication of the problem was called to my attention by Richard Betts.

27. A discussion of the relevant techniques for identifying the source of a weapon can be found in Charles A. Ziegler and David Jacobson, *Spying Without Spies* (New York: Praeger, 1995).

28. On the inherent difficulties of democracies' demonstrating resolve, see John Spanier and Eric M. Uslaner, *American Foreign Policy and the Democratic Dilemmas* (Belmont, Calif.: Brooks/Gage, 1989).

29. Such an argument for missile defenses is discussed in Robert Powell, "Nuclear Deterrence Theory, Nuclear Proliferation and National Missile Defense," *International Security* 27, no. 4 (Spring 2003): 86–118; and Victor Utgoff, "Proliferation, Missile Defense and American Ambitions," *Survival* 44, no. 2 (Summer 2002): 85–102.

30. On the impact of the media here, see Brigitte Linacos, Robert Y. Shapiro, and Pierangolo Isernia, *Decision Making in a Glass House: Mass Media, Public Opinion and American and European Foreign Policy in the 21st Century* (Lanham, Md.: Rowman and Littlefield, 2000).

31. This earlier nature of national interests with regard to alliances is discussed in Stephen M. Walt, *The Origins of Alliances* (Ithaca, N.Y.: Cornell University Press, 1987).

32. On the nature of post-1945 American alliance commitments, see Robert E. Osgood, *NATO: The Entangling Alliance* (Chicago: University of Chicago Press, 1962).

33. The breaking of the U.S.–New Zealand alliance is described in detail in Ewan Jamieson, *Friend or Ally: New Zealand at Odds with Its Past* (New York: Brassey's, 1990).

34. For a wide variety of arguments against national missile defense, see George Lewis, Lisbeth Gronlund, and David Wright, "National Missile Defense: An Indefensible System," *Foreign Policy*, no. 117 (Winter 1999–2000): 120–131; and John Newhouse, "The Missile Defense Debate," *Foreign Affairs* 80, no. 4 (July–August 2001): 97–109.

35. See Stephen M. Walt, "Containing Rogues and Renegades: Coalition Strategies and Counter-Proliferation," in Victor Utgoff, ed., *The Coming Crisis: Nuclear Proliferation, U.S. Interests and World Order* (Cambridge: MIT Press, 2000), pp. 191–226.

36. On the great variety of forms of terrorist organization, see Martha Crenshaw, *Terrorism in Context* (College Station: Pennsylvania State University Press, 1995); and Frederick Hacker, *Crusaders, Criminals, Crazies* (New York: W. W. Norton, 1976).

37. The importance of the actual events in the Japanese surrender for the future deterrent impact of nuclear weapons is discussed in Paul Fussell, "Thank God for the Atomic Bomb," reprinted in Kai Bird and Lawrence Lifschultz, eds., *Hiroshima's Shadow* (Stoney Creek, Conn.: Pamphleteer's Press, 1998).

38. Schelling, *Strategy of Conflict,* chap. 3.

39. The likely growth of North Korean nuclear capabilities is outlined in Robert Norris, "North Korea's Nuclear Program, 2003," *Bulletin of the Atomic Scientists* 59, no. 2 (February 2003): 74–78.

40. On the American diplomacy toward Israel during the Gulf War, see Rick Atkinson, *Crusade: The Untold Story of the Persian Gulf War* (Boston: Houghton-Mifflin, 1993).

41. For evidence of such reasoning within the George W. Bush administration, see Richard Sokolsky, "Demystifying the Nuclear Posture Review," *Survival* 44, no. 3 (Autumn 2002): 133–148.

42. On the moral and practical difficulties of nuclear target planning against the Soviet Union, see Steven P. Lee, *Morality, Prudence and Nuclear Weapons* (New York: Cambridge University Press, 1993).

43. The argument for a greater array of non-nuclear capabilities emerges from a number of the participants in the RAND "Day After" simulation, as described in Marc Dean Millot, Rogert Molander, and Peter Wilson, *"The Day After . . . " Study: Nuclear Proliferation in the Post–Cold War World* (Santa Monica, Calif.: RAND Corporation, 1993).

44. On "limited strategic nuclear war" between the United States and the Soviet Union, see Klaus Knorr and Thornton Read, eds., *Limited Strategic War* (Princeton, N.J.: Princeton University Press, 1962).

45. The arguments for an all-conventional response are in effect presented in Robert S. McNamara, "The Military Role of Nuclear Weapons," *Foreign Affairs* 62, no. 1 (Fall 1983): 59–80.

SIX: Some Final Observations

1. Edwin Hoyt, *Japan's War* (New York: McGraw-Hill, 1986) presents an analysis of Japanese strategic planning before Pearl Harbor.

2. On the inevitability of a double standard regarding nuclear proliferation, see Lewis Dunn, *Controlling the Bomb* (New Haven, Conn.: Yale University Press, 1982).

3. The general strategic implications of the September 11th attacks are laid out in "After 11 September," *Survival* 43, no. 4 (Winter 2001): 5–88.

4. For an analysis of the situation with India and Pakistan, see Neil Joeck, *Maintaining Nuclear Stability in South Asia,* Adelphi Paper No. 312 (London: IISS, 1997).

5. On the ins and outs of world respect for these "taboos," see Victor Utgoff, *The Challenge of Chemical Weapons* (London: Macmillan, 1990).

6. On the aftermath of the 1998 tests, see William Walker, "The Risks of Further Testing in South Asia," *Arms Control Today* 29, no. 6 (September–October 1999): 20–25.

7. On the likely growth of other WMD capabilities, see John E. Sopko, "The Changing Proliferation Threat," *Foreign Policy,* no. 105 (Winter 1996–1997): 3–20; and James Adams, "Virtual Defense," *Foreign Affairs* 80, no. 3 (May–June 2001): 98–113.

8. The accusation of racism can be found in Arjun Makitani, "Japan Always the Target," *Bulletin of the Atomic Scientists* 51, no. 3 (May–June 1995): 23–27.

9. That the United States would suffer a loss of international standing in most cases if a nuclear weapon were used by anyone was a conclusion that emerged generally from the RAND simulation, Marc Dean Millot, Roger Molander, and Peter Wilson, *"The Day After" . . . Study: Nuclear Proliferation in the Post–Cold War World* (Santa Monica, Calif.: RAND Corporation, 1993).

10. Examples of this kind of analysis can be found in Peter W. Rodman, "The World's Resentment: Anti-Americanism as a Global Phenomenon," *The National Interest*, no. 60 (Summer 2000): 33–41.

11. That the world in reality has been much more inclined to trust American power is asserted in François Heisbourg, "American Hegemony?: Perceptions of the U.S. Abroad," *Survival* 41, no. 4 (Winter 1999–2000): 5–19.

12. See, for example, Eric Nordlinger, *Isolationism Reconfigured* (Princeton, N.J.: Princeton University Press, 1995).

13. On the George W. Bush administration's initial proclamation of an aversion to being the world's policeman, see Condoleezza Rice, "Promoting the National Interest," *Foreign Affairs* 79, no. 1 (January–February 2000): 45–62.

14. Such a worrisome analysis of the impact of nuclear proliferation could be extracted from the results of the RAND "Day After" simulation, Millot, Molander, and Wilson, *"The Day After . . . " Study*.

15. On the negative consequences of a weakening of the American commitment to Japan, see John H. Miller, "The Glacier Moves: Japan's Response to U.S. Security Policies," *Asian Affairs* 30, no. 2 (Summer 2003): 132–141.

Index

132, 138–139; impact of nuclear weapons use on, 67–70, 71–73, 86, 123

rationality, 6, 7, 39–41, 42, 49, 121
"rogue states," 7, 18, 24, 41, 46–51, 59, 81, 102, 111–117
Russia, 3, 11, 26, 41, 45, 48, 49, 51, 57, 58, 60, 62, 63, 66, 67, 72, 83, 85, 93, 100, 102, 105, 108, 113, 120, 127, 136

Saddam Hussein, 3, 4, 58, 59, 64–65, 77, 91, 117, 136
Saudi Arabia, 46
Schelling, Thomas, 32, 34, 115
September 11, 2001, terrorist attacks, 3–4, 5, 14, 15, 16, 26, 36, 38–39, 42, 54, 55, 58, 62, 65, 70, 80, 85–88, 111, 113, 128, 132, 137
simulations of nuclear escalation scenarios, 17–18
Somalia, 70
South Africa, 25, 48, 75
Soviet Union, 29, 31–32, 37, 41, 46–47, 49, 56, 57, 69, 72, 77, 93, 96, 97, 100, 104, 105, 111, 115, 122–123, 128–129

taboos, 2, 4, 12–16, 18, 23, 24, 26, 28, 29, 30, 32–33, 35–36, 38, 42, 43, 53–55, 65, 67, 72, 75–76, 95, 108, 110, 112, 118, 130, 133, 139
tactical nuclear weapons, 8, 18–19, 31, 34–36, 53, 85–86
Taiwan, 8–9, 35, 48, 71, 78

Taliban, 39, 62, 112–113
terrorists: nuclear weapons use against, 19, 34, 75; nuclear weapons use by, 3, 7–8, 12, 24, 30, 36–39, 41–42, 56, 76, 104–105, 127, 129; state-sponsored, 38–39, 76
testing, nuclear, 3, 7, 13–14, 15, 29–30, 85–86, 95, 106, 123–124
theater missile defense (TMD), 36, 69, 79

United States: intervention abroad by, 4, 5, 7–9, 50, 69, 77, 81–82, 84–85, 105, 109, 112, 118, 120, 137–138; isolationism of, 57–59, 61–62, 78–79, 82, 88, 107–111, 132, 137; as next user of nuclear weapons, 8, 11, 17, 32–33, 35, 51, 76, 84, 86–87, 100, 101–102, 103, 123–126, 132, 134–135, 136–137; resolve of, 3, 70, 72–73, 77–89, 93, 103, 108–110, 137; unilateralism of, 58–59, 82, 85, 112; world leadership by, 44–45, 58–59, 61–64, 91–92, 134–138

Vietnam, 49
Vietnam War, 88, 134

weapons of mass destruction (WMD), 4, 12, 15, 17, 19, 21–23, 45, 69, 100–102, 113, 123–125, 132, 133. *See also* chemical and biological weapons
World War I, 5, 77, 79, 83, 131
World War II, 1, 4, 10, 12, 14, 15, 34, 42, 65, 71, 77, 81, 83, 87–88, 109, 114, 115, 124–125, 127, 134, 135
World War III, 1, 18, 47, 51–52, 105